MONDAY MORNING QUARTER- BACK

Jim Benagh, Fred Charrow and Sid Lerner

An Owl Book

HOLT, RINEHART AND WINSTON
New York

Written by Jim Benagh
Designed and illustrated by Fred Charrow

Copyright © 1983 by Sid Lerner Associates, Inc.
All rights reserved, including the right to reproduce this
book or portions thereof in any form.
Published by Holt, Rinehart and Winston,
383 Madison Avenue, New York, New York 10017.
Published simultaneously in Canada by Holt, Rinehart and
Winston of Canada, Limited.

Library of Congress Cataloging in Publication Data

Benagh, Jim, 1937–
Monday morning quarterback.
1. Football—Miscellanea. I. Charrow, Fred.
II. Lerner, Sid. III. Title.
GV951.15.B46 1983   796.332   83-12650

ISBN: 0-03-063776-7

Editorial production by Harkavy Publishing Service

First Edition

Printed in the United States of America
10 9 8 7 6 5 4 3 2 1

ISBN 0-03-063776-7

CONTENTS

The play's the thing. . . .
        Shakespeare
        Hamlet

But which one?
        The editors
        Monday Morning Quarterback

MONDAY MORNING QUARTER- BACK

Few things in the history of the world have changed a day of the week as football has changed Monday. It used to be a dull day, the first in a series of layovers until the next weekend began. But professional football has changed that, at least in the United States. Monday is now the day to recap the professional football games, to collect or pay the bets, to await "Monday Night Football," and, in general, to talk strategy on how your team won or lost its last game.

People find themselves talking in football terminology: "quarterbacking the sales force," "blitzing the market," or "sending one of the office boys on an end run for coffee."

But the major topic of conversation, in season, is football and the strategy of the game itself.

There is no better way to learn than to sit down and analyze the games as they are going on, helped by instant replays and expert commentators. Before long, even the novice thinks he can quarterback a game.

The idea of this book is to present that strategy in actual game conditions from the 1982 season, playoffs, and Super Bowl. We have selected 100 plays—not just game-breaking touchdowns but busted plays, sacks, dropped passes, and so on. But the big plays are here, and they come from a season of razzle-dazzle football unlike any ever seen in the National Football League (NFL), for the short season wasn't short on new or offbeat strategy.

The best way for the reader to use this book is to read the situation first and then call your own play—before trying to guess what the team is going to do.

The plays we've chosen were taken from game films, videotapes, and long talks with coaches and football experts. An effort has been made to present the plays as they actually happened, though in some cases the times that plays began have been estimated and pass and running routes of some of the players have been approximated, particularly if those players were in secondary roles.

We are deeply indebted to Art Berke of ABC Television, Kevin Monaghan of NBC Television, and Doug Richardson and Mike DelNagro of CBS Television. Two football coaches who were of particular help were Rusty Tillman of the Seattle Seahawks and Maxie Baughan, former Detroit Lion assistant who is now head coach at Cornell University.

Jim Benagh
Fred Charrow
Sid Lerner

A PRIMER
history of offensive football strategy

Those American football fans who watched the Washington Redskins win Super Bowl XVII in January 1983 with a startling array of men-in-motion plays would have turned off their television sets in boredom if they had been watching a game in the first recorded year of professional football—1892.

For years, as American football evolved from English rugby, the wedge was football's offense. In his 1891 book *American Football*, author Walter Camp explained: "The wedge, or V, is the play used to open a game by probably nine-tenths of the teams." It consisted of an open or closed V pointed at the opposition, with the ballcarrier tucked in the middle, to be pushed, pulled, or guided by his teammates as the wedge moved forward. Occasionally, the man in the middle could, at his discretion, try to sneak out of the wedge and run on his own. Or he could go straight forward if the wedge opened up a hole in the opponents' defense. At other times, the offense would form a diagonal line that would allow the runner to progress forward.

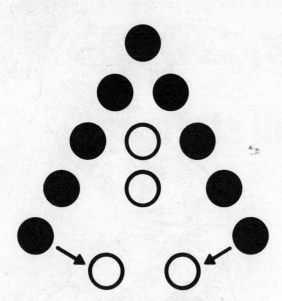

THE WEDGE

The V-shaped wedge could be converged at the ends if opponents tried to get in from behind; this way, a mass of bodies, with the ballcarrier enveloped inside, would try to push forward.

FLYING WEDGE

In a variation of the wedge called the flying wedge, two groups of players would come flying at full speed and provide an impact on opponents as they converged around the ballcarrier.

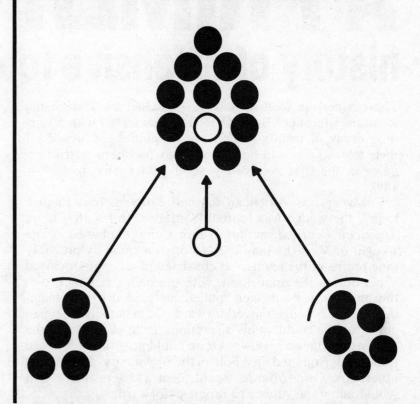

T-FORMATION

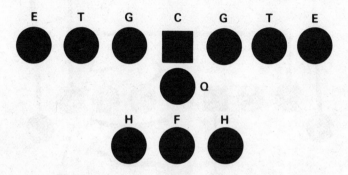

The original T-formation is pretty much the basis for almost all the strategies that followed, and it also gave football something on which to base the names of the different positions. In the late 1940s, it was the formation from which Notre Dame dominated football and the one that most high school and professional teams adopted.

For almost a half century, one of the most popular football formations—for high schools, colleges, and professionals—was the single-wing formation. It began as a power formation; hence, the unbalanced line mostly to the right. But in later years, until it virtually faded out in the 1950s, the single wing included many sophisticated passing and reverse plays mixed in with the power runs by the tailback and fullback.

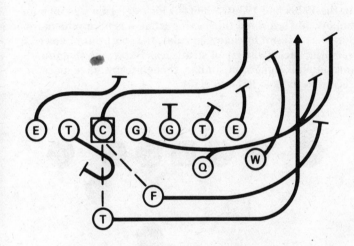

SINGLE WING

SHORT PUNT

In the 1920s and 1930s, when the kicking game was such an important factor and the passing game was becoming more of a staple as a result of changing rules, the short punt allowed a versatile back a variety of strategies. Today, the shotgun formation is somewhat similar, though teams have more receivers flanked left and right.

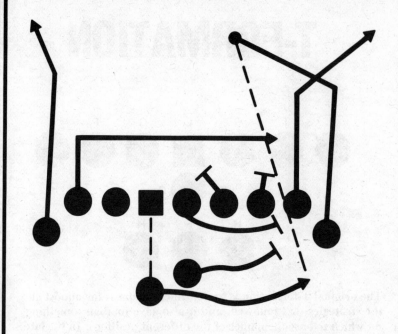

Pop Warner used this formation when he coached Jim Thorpe at Carlisle, and he made it more popular at Stanford University in the 1920s. It made for more open passing attacks.

DOUBLE WING

MAN-IN-MOTION

The Chicago Bears, under George Halas, began using the man-in-motion about 1930. The Bears ran it from their T-formation.

SINGLE WING

DOUBLE WING

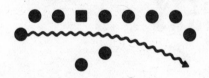

T-FORMATION

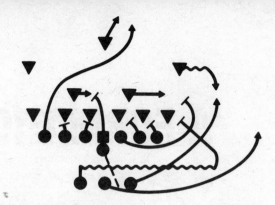

BEARS' "T"

The Chicago Bears refined the T-formation to make it more adaptable to the professionals, who had more skills and more time to develop plays. Players like Sammy Baugh gave the T instant recognition and elevated the status of the professional quarterback to the heights he enjoys today.

BAUGH PASSES

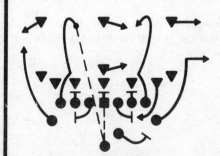

A-FORMATION

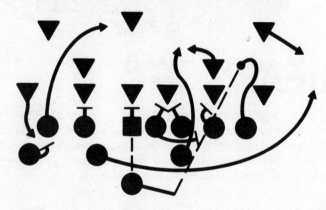

This formation was developed by Steve Owens, the famous coach of the New York Giants. It split the running backs out farther than they had been.

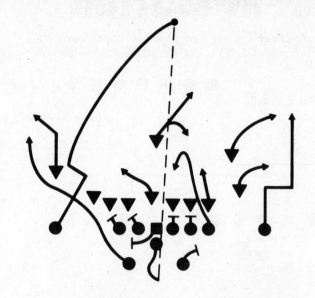

RAMS' BOMB

Elroy Hirsch and the other long threats hired by the Los Angeles Rams encouraged the team to come up with plays to utilize their special talents.

PRO SETS

These different patterns allowed teams with several good receivers to add variety to the offenses of the 1950s and 1960s.

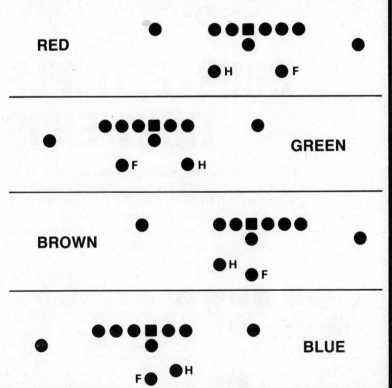

RED

GREEN

BROWN

BLUE

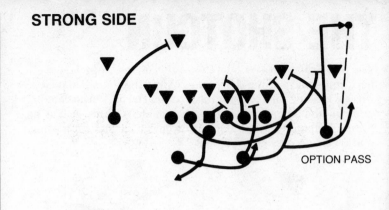

STRONG SIDE

OPTION PASS

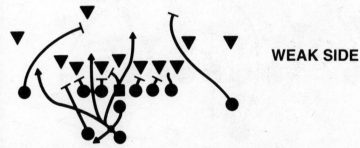

WEAK SIDE

GREEN BAY SWEEPS

When Coach Vince Lombardi, a master at teaching the running game and blocking, was coach at Green Bay, he made use of his running tandem of Paul Hornung and Jim Taylor, who could both block and run. With blockers like Jerry Kramer and Fuzzy Thurston as the power blockers and pulling guards, the Packer sweeps were devastating.

THE SHOTGUN

The San Francisco 49ers developed this offense, which goes back to the days of the short punt. While the 49ers had mixed success looking for the right modern quarterback who could also run and adapt to its uniqueness, modern teams such as the Miami Dolphins and the Dallas Cowboys have made it a winner under certain passing conditions.

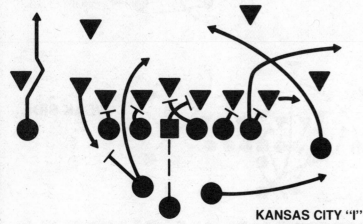

KANSAS CITY "I"

The Kansas City Chiefs, in their heyday in the 1960s, used this formation to spring loose such little backs as Mike Garrett. The "I" back is the one farthest back, and a fullback-type blocker sets right in front of him.

DOUBLE, TRIPLE TIGHT ENDS

This is the offense of the 1980s, as practiced by the Super Bowl XVII championship Washington Redskins. It has been said that the tight end (Y) is the player of the future—that is, until pro football changes its ever-changing style one more time. (X and Z are wide receivers.)

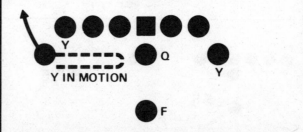

Y IN MOTION

FIRST QUARTER

THE 9-WEEK SEASON

1ST QUARTER

In the course of a normal NFL season—28 teams each playing 16 regular-season games—about 27,000 plays are run from scrimmage. Even in the strike-shortened, nine-week 1982 season, more than 15,000 passes and rushes were tried.

Despite fewer games, 1982 was not lacking in excitement. Indeed, some observers of professional football said that NFL teams opened up their offenses more than usual; in a hectic nine-game season, a couple of big plays could win a couple of big games, even one game, and it took less than a .500 season to make the playoffs in at least a couple of cases. Teams that normally would go through a conservative pattern over the usual 16-game season, figuring that talent would win out in the long run, were installing an array of flea-flickers, end-around runs, halfback passes, reverses, and double reverses—plays that have always been used but in 1982 seemed to be used with more frequency. For teams with lesser aspirations at the start of the strike-bound season, wide-open attacks and game plans increased the chances of getting a playoff berth in the expanded 16-team playoffs. One team even used a quick-kick punt to win a game.

From those 15,000 or so plays in the 126 regular-season games, the editors have selected some of the more significant plays—many of them unusual—from what turned out to be both a significant and unusual season.

THE SEASON

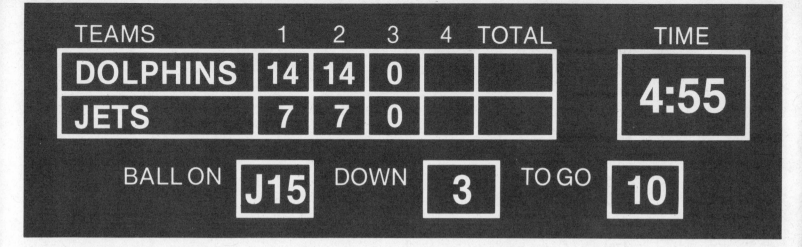

TEAMS	1	2	3	4	TOTAL	TIME
DOLPHINS	14	14	0			
JETS	7	7	0			4:55

BALL ON **J15** DOWN **3** TO GO **10**

THE SITUATION   The Miami Dolphins, a playoff team the season before, are opening the season against a real nemesis, the New York Jets, who have beaten the Dolphins seven times and tied them once in the last eight meetings. Despite the down and yardage, the Dolphins are looking for the big play that could probably break the Jets and end their domination of the past few years.

In this game, which Jets Coach Walt Michaels later described as a ''comedy of errors,'' the Dolphins are holding the powerful Jet front four to no sacks and running the ball well, especially when powerful Andra Franklin has the assignment. David Woodley,

the Miami quarterback, has been sharing the signal calling with Don Strock over the previous season's games but has the assignment on this play. He is versatile, and by lining up in the shotgun formation, the Dolphins have a lot of options. Duriel Harris and Jimmy Cefalo are good receivers in such a situation because they both run many patterns. Tony Nathan is a more likely running back this close to the goal line with third-and-10 yardage because he is a more wide-open back.

Unless you get the first down, you will probably have to settle for a field-goal attempt. What do you try?

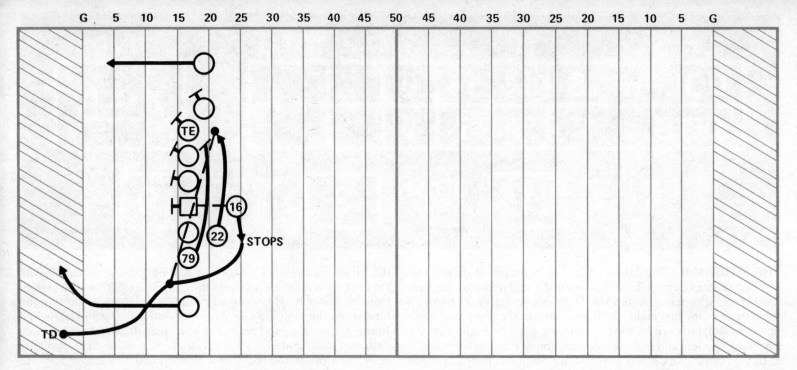

THE DECISION The call is for a flea-flicker, a make-or-break big play. Woodley (16) is in the shotgun, with Nathan (22) his only deep back. The play is designed to get the Jets to believe Nathan will take a short lateral from Woodley and spring around the strong side, led by the pulling left tackle, Jon Giesler (79). But the actual play is for Nathan to stop short and pivot and hit Woodley in the left flat, where he has casually moved into position after getting the ball to Nathan.

THE RESULT After getting the ball to Nathan, Woodley stepped off to the left, as quarterbacks often do. The Jets, watching the strong-side blocking develop, and perhaps mesmerized by Giesler pulling to lead Nathan, shifted in that direction. Meanwhile, Woodley floated over to the scrimmage line by the time Nathan pivoted and set to pass. The pass was good, and Woodley had an open field to the end zone, taking advantage of it to ice the game. The Dolphins scored two more quick touchdowns in the quarter and won, 45–28.

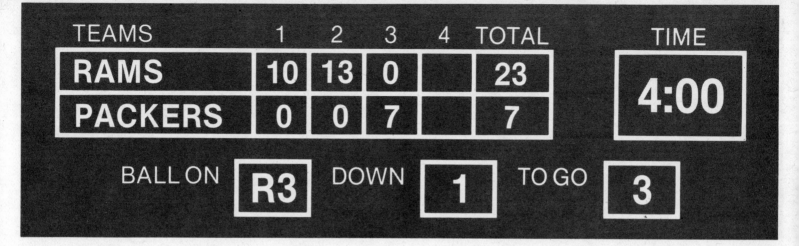

TEAMS	1	2	3	4	TOTAL	TIME
RAMS	10	13	0		23	4:00
PACKERS	0	0	7		7	

BALL ON **R3** DOWN **1** TO GO **3**

THE SITUATION A couple of frustrated 1981 teams try to re-group in their 1982 opener, at Milwaukee's County Stadium. Both missed the playoffs the season before, Green Bay in the final game and the Rams for the first time since 1972.

The Packers' frustration seems to be continuing, however, as they are down, 23–7, late in the third quarter and desperately need a touchdown. They have run the ball on virtually every first-down play in the half, though they got on the scoreboard for the first time when they ended an 85-yard drive with a 4-yard touchdown pass to the tight end Paul Coffman. On this drive, Coffman's 42-yard catch from Lynn Dickey was the key play so

far. Dickey's passing has been hampered by interceptions this day, however. Coffman complements an explosive pass-catching trio that also includes John Jefferson and James Lofton as the wide receivers. Eddie Lee Ivery is the team's best and most dangerous rusher, and his knee, after two operations in three years, seems sound again. His runs this game have been either long or small-gainers. Gerry Ellis, the fullback, is a promising player who averages more than 4 yards a carry.

You've got four downs, but time is becoming a factor, and a touchdown is a must. What is your call?

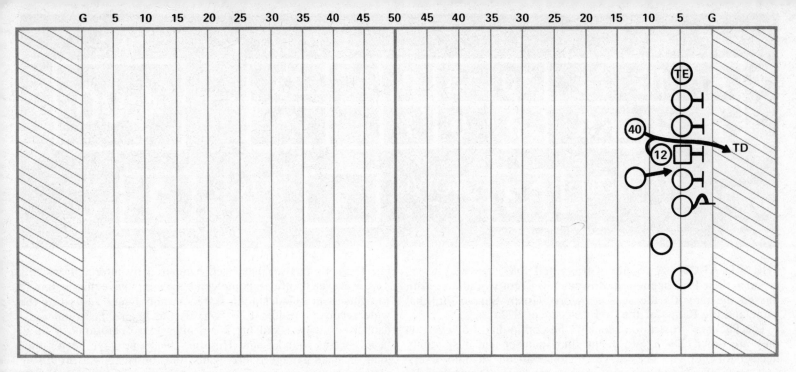

THE DECISION   The Packers go with their best back, Ivery (40), on a simple power play in which he takes the handoff from Dickey (12) and heads into the line to the left of the center. Nothing fancy; just make use of Ivery's running talent.

THE RESULT   Touchdown. It didn't eat up a lot of time, and subsequently the Packers got their passing game into the groove as Dickey connected for short touchdown strikes to Lofton (15 yards) and Coffman (10 yards) to go ahead after being behind, 23–0. Ivery's final touchdown run made the final score: Packers 35, Rams 23.

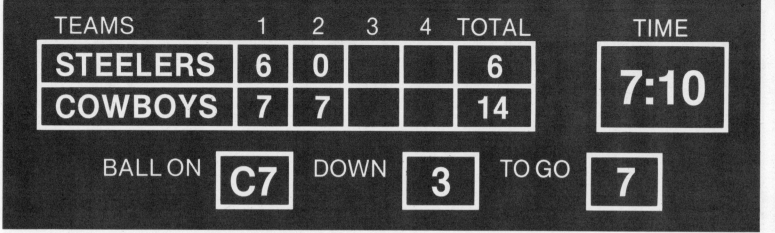

TEAMS	1	2	3	4	TOTAL
STEELERS	6	0			6
COWBOYS	7	7			14

TIME 7:10

BALL ON C7 DOWN 3 TO GO 7

THE SITUATION Two tough teams of the 1970s—the Dallas Cowboys and the Pittsburgh Steelers—are carrying their talent into the 1980s in the season's first Monday night game. The Steelers came in with a 4–0 record in preseason play; the Cowboys, 3–1. After a missed extra point in the first period, the Steelers are down in scoring territory, but it is long yardage on third down. A short run that fails only gives the Steelers field-goal position; a pass could mean an interception. But the Steelers, with receivers like John Stallworth, Lynn Swann, Bennie Cunningham, Calvin Sweeney, and Jim Smith, can throw the ball. Terry Bradshaw has been in this situation before, many a time, and many a time has been successful. With Franco Harris, the league's third all-time rusher going into the game, and Frank Pollard, coming off a season in which he gained 570 yards, the Steelers are sound on the ground, too.

Third and 7 yards, and you need the touchdown to get back in the game. What's the call?

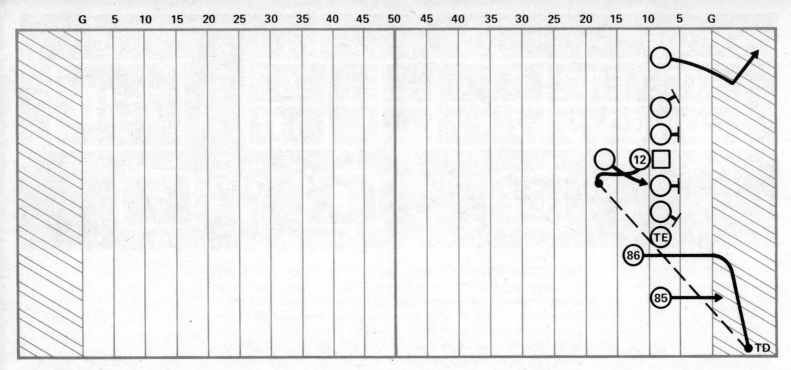

THE DECISION Bradshaw (12) goes to the air, on a play aimed for Smith (86), one of football's underrated receivers. Smith has been in the shadows of Swann and Stallworth for a few years, but coming out of the slot, he is a dangerous man, short or long. The play calls for Smith to go into the end zone a yard or two, then cut to the corner. Sweeney (85) is to go into the end zone, too.

THE RESULT A touchdown for Smith, who made the catch in the corner of the end zone, as planned. Classic Bradshaw pass, based on talent at both ends and other possible options. (Another play in this game follows.)

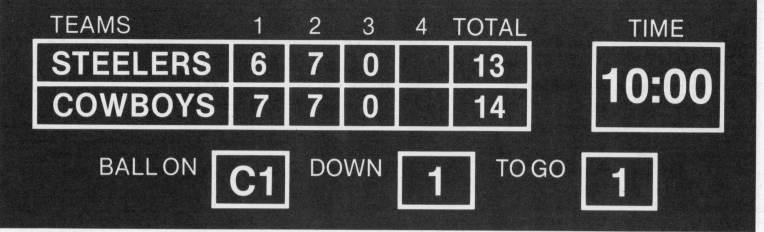

TEAMS	1	2	3	4	TOTAL
STEELERS	6	7	0		13
COWBOYS	7	7	0		14

TIME 10:00

BALL ON C1 DOWN 1 TO GO 1

THE SITUATION The Steelers have a chance to go ahead for the first time since the opening period, and they are clicking offensively. Franco Harris is getting his share of yardage, and Frank Pollard is complementing him at the other running-back spot with decent yardage, though not carrying the ball as much. The Steelers also have Russell Davis, a good short-yardage backup for Harris, on hold, if they need him. While the Steelers don't get too fancy down here in this kind of situation, they do have the receivers who can get the ball in the end zone—Bennie Cunningham, the tight end, and Jim Smith, coming out of the slot, are two of them.

Undoubtedly, a running situation on first down and an almost easy touchdown, but who do you run and where do you run him?

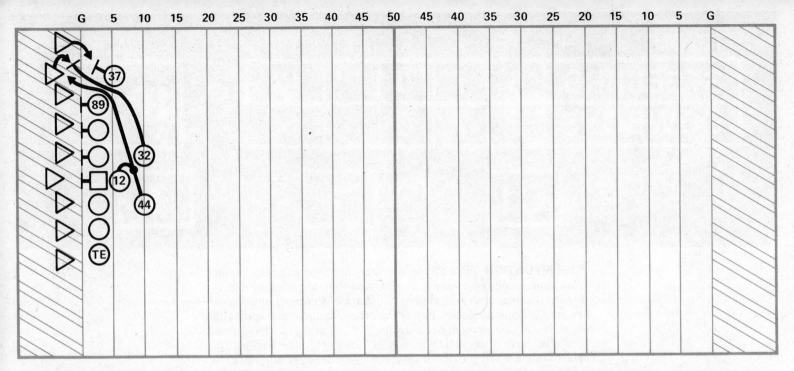

THE DECISION Normally, one might just expect a smack up the middle, using either Harris (32), Pollard (44), or even Davis (45). But the Steelers chose to run Pollard around the right tight end, Cunningham (89), using some power blocks by Frank Wilson (37), a combination tight end-running back, and Harris.

THE RESULT A Steeler touchdown on an unconventional play but conventional Pittsburgh success. The key blockers came through on this one. The Steelers went on to win the game after another touchdown catch by Smith and three field goals. The 36–28 Pittsburgh victory ended the Cowboys' string of 17 straight opening-game triumphs, an NFL record.

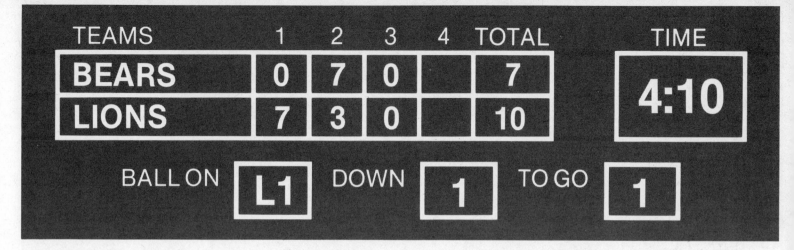

TEAMS	1	2	3	4	TOTAL	TIME
BEARS	0	7	0		7	4:10
LIONS	7	3	0		10	

BALL ON **L1**   DOWN **1**   TO GO **1**

THE SITUATION   Though it is opening game for both teams at the Silverdome in Pontiac, Michigan, both the Detroit Lions and Chicago Bears are already mired in quarterback problems. Gary Danielson would come in for relief of Eric Hipple, whose Lion offense was plodding for most of the game, and Bob Avellini of the Bears went out with a nasty mouth cut in the first half, being replaced by Vince Evans, his backup. Neither team is moving the ball very well, and in the third quarter, the game is still up for grabs.

But the Bears have a chance to go ahead in the third quarter, the result of a drive that begins in midquarter on their own 29. The Bears, with the help of an interference penalty, have first down on the Lions' 1-yard line.

In this game, neither of the Bears' top runners—Walter Payton or Matt Suhey—has made inroads on the artificial turf. They have gained only about 2 yards a carry, which was the distance of Suhey's early scoring plunge. Avellini's passing is next to nil, but he is back in the game in the crucial goal-line situation. Emery Moorehead, the tight end, is good in up-close situations. Payton, one of the leading rushers in NFL history, can catch, too.

It seems so basic. What's your choice of play?

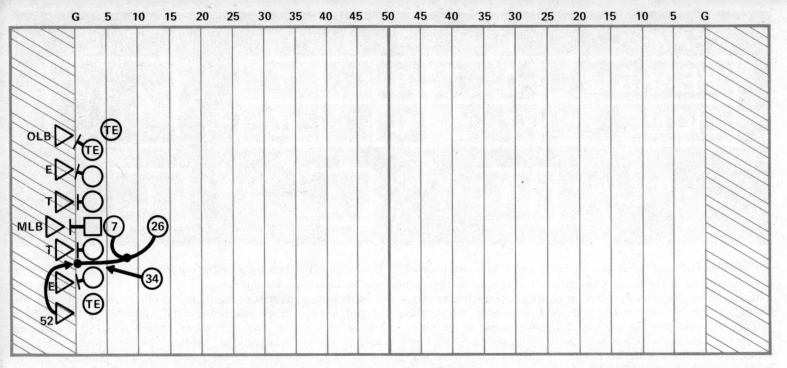

THE DECISION The Bears line up with Avellini (7) at quarterback over the center. Suhey (26) is at fullback, about 4 yards behind Avellini. Payton (34) lines up at halfback to the left. There are three tight ends in the game, including one at the wing to the strong side. The call is for Payton to lead Suhey through a hole over left tackle.

THE RESULT A couple of feet, but not a full yard, and the Bears end up inches short. Stan White (52), the Lions' weak-side linebacker, who was lined up on the line right across from the Bears' left tight end, broke through and made the tackle. That left the Bears with second down and inches to go. (The next play in this series follows.)

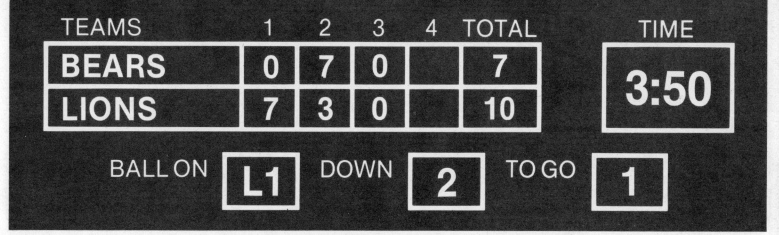

TEAMS	1	2	3	4	TOTAL	TIME
BEARS	0	7	0		7	3:50
LIONS	7	3	0		10	

BALL ON **L1**   DOWN **2**   TO GO **1**

THE SITUATION   Keep in mind that the Bears confront virtually the same situation as the previous play when they make their decision except that they are dealing with inches instead of a yard and that it is second down. Looks like a piece of cake and that all the coach has to do is decide whom he wants to give a gift touchdown to.

So who gets the ball?

Avellini and Evans, the other quarterback, can both run the ball. Avellini averaged 35 carries a season in his role as starter a couple of seasons during the 1970s. Evans rushed 60 times, for a 5.1-yard average, in 1980.

Payton is Payton, a sure Hall of Famer.

Suhey is at his best smacking into the line, and he already has that 2-yard touchdown this day.

Passing, of course, would be silly and dangerous.

Draw straws? Give it to anybody? Or make a solid choice?

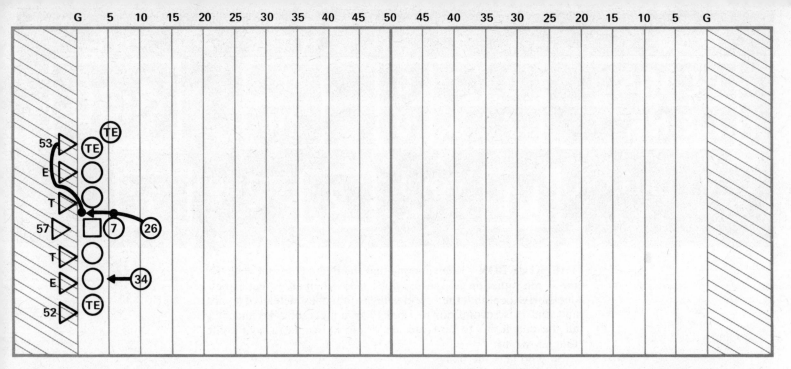

THE DECISION The Bears want to line up the same way as on the previous play, with Suhey (26) again getting the ball, but this time more straight ahead because of the need for just inches. Avellini (7) stays in at quarterback, and Payton (34) is the running back. The call is for Suhey to go over right guard.

THE RESULT The Lions also are lined in their previous formation, except that the middle linebacker, Ken Fantetti (57), is only about 1½ yards from the center instead of 3½ yards, as on the first-down play. As Avellini turns to make the handoff to Suhey, Garry Cobb (53), the Lions' left linebacker, who had been playing over the strong-side tight end, is there to meet him. Cobb tackles Suhey on the spot, again an inch or so from the goal line. (The next play in this series follows.)

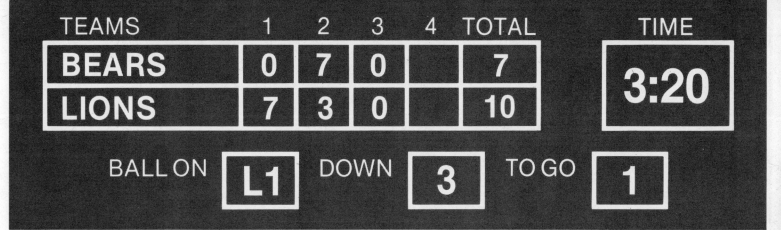

TEAMS	1	2	3	4	TOTAL
BEARS	0	7	0		7
LIONS	7	3	0		10

TIME 3:20

BALL ON **L1** DOWN **3** TO GO **1**

THE SITUATION Pretty much the same as the last time, one more time. The easiest call in football is getting more complicated. The Lions just are not budging, much less buckling in the line. With their tackles pinching in on the center, there is no room for Avellini to move forward.

Do you try something different again?

Suhey is still the best man, statistically and strategically, in such situations. He is small but a compact runner.

Payton is even smaller, not much over 200 pounds, but has years of experience and literally miles of yardage as a rusher.

Bring in Evans? Let Avellini give it a shot up the middle?

A pass? A different formation?

Your guess.

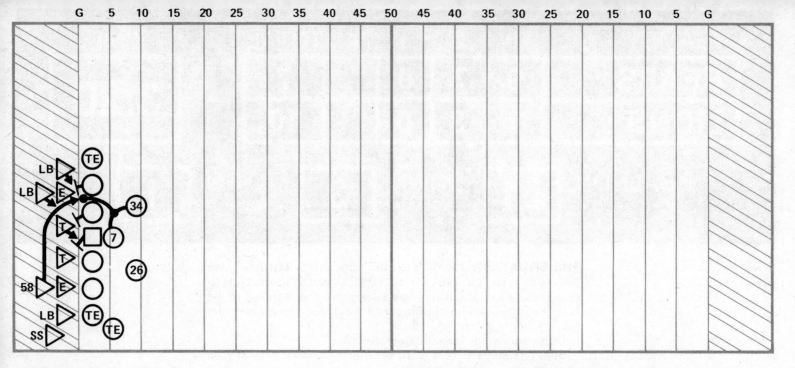

| G | 5 | 10 | 15 | 20 | 25 | 30 | 35 | 40 | 45 | 50 | 45 | 40 | 35 | 30 | 25 | 20 | 15 | 10 | 5 | G |

THE DECISION   Payton.

The Bears, however, first go into a different formation, with Suhey (26) to the left and Payton (34) squared off across from him on the right side, both just about 4 yards behind the tackles. The extra tight end on the wing goes to the left side on this play. There are still two tight ends on the line. The call is for Avellini (7) to hand off to Payton on the dive over right tackle.

THE RESULT   Lions' linebackers 3, Bears ballcarriers 0.

Steve Doig (58) barreled through the area vacated by the left tackle and into Payton, who tried to dive over the line. With some help from a pile of teammates, Doig held Payton short of the goal line, forcing the Bears into a fourth down. (The next play in this series follows.)

TEAMS	1	2	3	4	TOTAL	TIME
BEARS	0	7	0		7	3:00
LIONS	7	3	0		10	

BALL ON L1 **DOWN** 4 **TO GO** 1

THE SITUATION Despite the exercise so far in what has been called Neanderthal football, most coaches would love to have fourth down and less than a foot, with a chance for the go-ahead touchdown. The Bears could even get a tying field goal here, though that would seem bad strategy after a long drive and in the first game of the season.

The options remain the same, as they have for three previous plays.

At this juncture, do you use something cute? Something different—a rollout, a change in quarterback, some fresh faces in the running-back position, something to spread out the defense?

Or do you stay with the same old stuff?

What is your call?

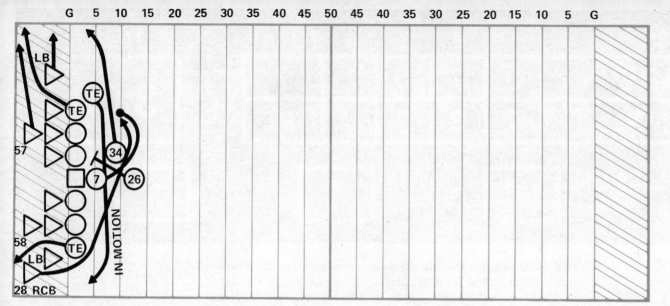

THE DECISION   Avellini (7) stays in the game and tries a passing play out of a rollout. He has Suhey (26) back to block for him on the rollout to the right and Payton (34) going off to the sideline on the right. A tight end being used at wingback heads for the left side of the line, and the right tight end goes to the deep right corner. The left tight end goes toward the left corner.

THE RESULT   Avellini went behind Suhey, who was set up to block and was about 8 yards behind the line of scrimmage when he decided to turn and try to hit the wingback–tight end. But boom! James Hunter (28), the right cornerback, came through the area vacated by the left tight end and behind Suhey, who was blocking to the opposite side of the line, and Hunter smacked Avellini for a 10-yard loss.

End of opportunity.

The Lions got another touchdown, the Bears a field goal, and Detroit won the game, 17–10.

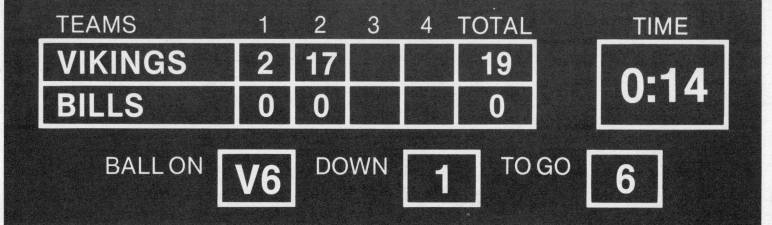

TEAMS	1	2	3	4	TOTAL	TIME
VIKINGS	2	17			19	0:14
BILLS	0	0			0	

BALL ON **V6** DOWN **1** TO GO **6**

THE SITUATION The Buffalo Bills, playing at home as well as in front of a national television audience on Monday night, are in the process of getting embarrassed. Though the Bills have the ball on the Minnesota Vikings' 6-yard line in a first-and-goal situation, the clock is working against the Bills, and a field goal won't bite into the Minnesota lead that much if this play doesn't result in a touchdown. Joe Ferguson, the Buffalo quarterback, is passing well and often, the latter because of Minnesota's big lead. Jerry Butler and Frank Lewis are excellent receivers, and Mark Brammer, the tight end, is solid. Ferguson likes to throw to a lot of different players.

Roosevelt Leaks, the top Buffalo running back, is having a decent night, though Joe Cribbs, the best back, has not yet returned to the team as a result of his holdout. Curtis Brown, starting at running back, can catch the ball, too.

Name a play in a hurry, because time is running out and the Bills need a touchdown.

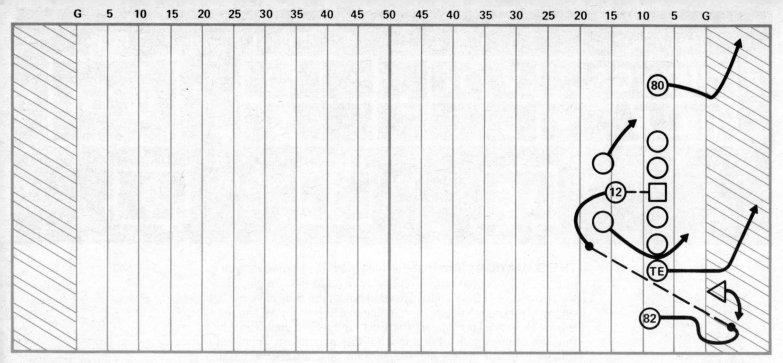

THE DECISION   Ferguson (12), the quarterback, goes into the shotgun, with his running backs off to his sides, though slightly in back of him. His play is to roll right, behind the right halfback, and try to catch a man downfield. Lewis (82) is to head downfield, break right just before the goal line, then go a few yards into the end zone, hooking inward.

THE RESULT   With receivers like Butler (80) and Lewis maneuvering in the end zone and a confident passer like Ferguson putting the ball in the air even in a tight corner, there was hope. Ferguson's pass was on target, a few yards into the end zone, and Buffalo got the touchdown. (Another play in this game follows.)

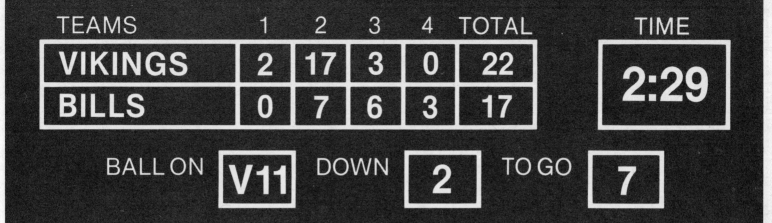

TEAMS	1	2	3	4	TOTAL	TIME
VIKINGS	2	17	3	0	22	
BILLS	0	7	6	3	17	**2:29**

BALL ON V11 **DOWN** 2 **TO GO** 7

THE SITUATION Buffalo is still behind in the game, right down to the wire. But Joe Ferguson has the Bills on the move against Minnesota. In seven plays, he has driven his team 83 yards to the second-and-7 point with little more than two minutes left in the game. Roosevelt Leaks has been having a decent night as a rusher, but is time getting too short to try pounding away against a good defense? Ferguson, with a 300-plus-yards night already, has completed more than half his passes, not for great yardage but respectable statistics. Frank Lewis has averaged 20 yards a catch on his four receptions so far, and Jerry Butler has come out of the first-half doldrums—he was shut out—to catch six passes for 100 yards in the second half.

A chance for Buffalo to go ahead, and there may not be any chances left after this series of downs. So how do you instruct your quarterback?

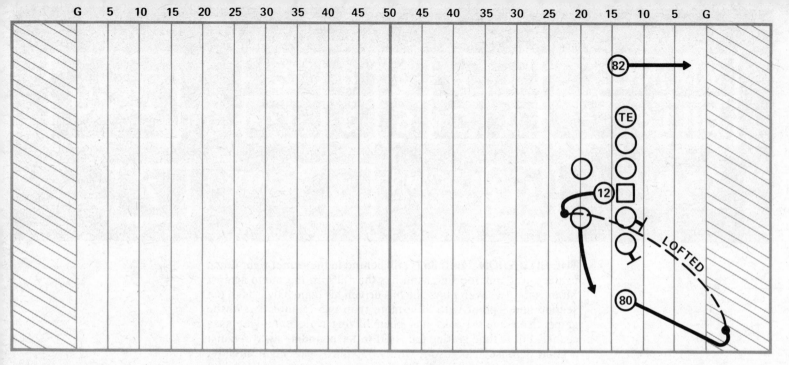

THE DECISION The Bills instruct Ferguson (12) to go for Butler (80) on a pass after a rollout. Because Butler is going almost straight ahead and is in a rush to get into the end zone, Ferguson's pass has to be quick.

THE RESULT Ferguson whipped the ball off quickly, lofting it over the right side of the line. Butler took the ball over his left shoulder as he was veering a little to the right, caught it, and the Bills had a stunning comeback victory, 23–22.

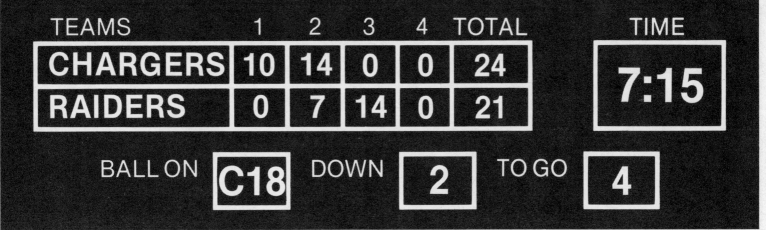

TEAMS	1	2	3	4	TOTAL
CHARGERS	10	14	0	0	24
RAIDERS	0	7	14	0	21

TIME 7:15

BALL ON **C18** DOWN **2** TO GO **4**

THE SITUATION The Los Angeles Raiders went into this game undefeated, while the San Diego Chargers did not yet have their high-gear offense revved up. A wide-open game was expected, as is the norm when these teams play, and they certainly were explosive up to this point. The Raiders had come back from a 24–0 deficit at one point in the first half and were now threatening to go in front of San Diego for the first time in the game. The Raiders have a first-class rookie, Marcus Allen, for situations like this, if you want to run him. Allen has shown he can catch the short passes, too. Todd Christensen, the tight end, has been Jim Plunkett's favorite target in this game, however. Cliff Branch has only caught two passes and Malcolm Barnwell, the other wide receiver, only one. But there are lots of options on this play, so choose one.

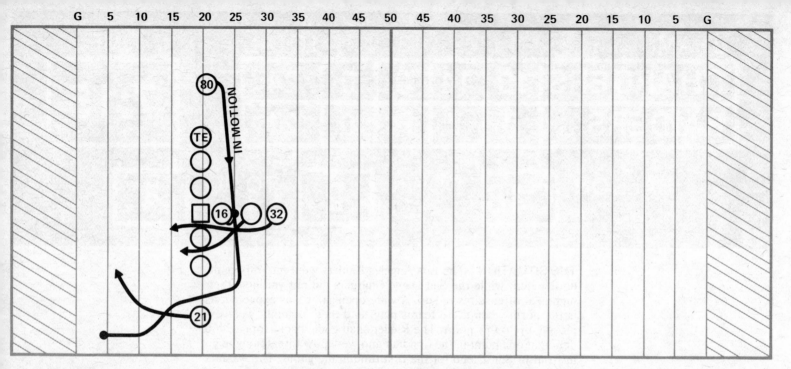

THE DECISION Both Marcus Allen (32) and Kenny King have lugged the ball often in this game, so Allen, coming from the deep back, is going to draw a crowd going into the line. Jim Plunkett's (16) call, however, is to fake to Allen and give to Malcolm Barnwell (80), coming around on the reverse. Cliff Branch (21) cuts into the center of the Chargers' defensive backfield to draw the crowd away from Barnwell's running area.

THE RESULT An exceptional job by Barnwell that netted the Raiders 14 yards and got them a first down on the Chargers' 4-yard line. From there they ran the ball in and defeated the Chargers, 28–24.

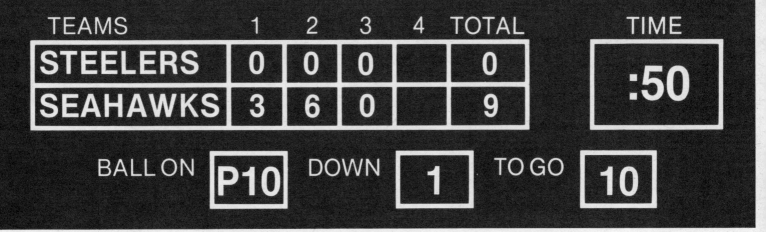

TEAMS	1	2	3	4	TOTAL	TIME
STEELERS	0	0	0		0	:50
SEAHAWKS	3	6	0		9	

BALL ON **P10** DOWN **1** TO GO **10**

THE SITUATION The Steelers came into this game looking like gangbusters, having won all three games they played. The Seahawks were near the bottom rung but were showing some improvement. Now, in the third quarter, Seattle was on the way to scoring just about the biggest upset, if not the biggest, in its seven-year history. A touchdown here would just about assure that. But despite their 9–0 lead, the Seahawks have yet to push across a touchdown in this game. Jim Zorn, the Seattle quarterback, is passing well but not for the big yards. The running game is sound but not overwhelming. The Steelers are explosive, so a field goal would only put the Seahawks up, 12–0, and still make them vulnerable. Where do you start in your quest for a touchdown after driving 58 yards?

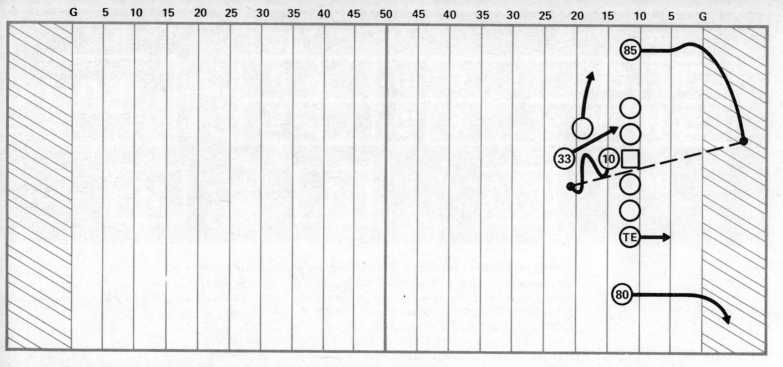

THE DECISION The Seahawks took to the air. Jim Zorn (10) set up his throw to Paul Johns (85) with a quick fake to Dan Doornink (33), then has to make the turn and the quick throw to Johns coming over the Steelers' backfield.

THE RESULT Johns made the touchdown, and the Seahawks held on to post a shocking 16–0 upset.

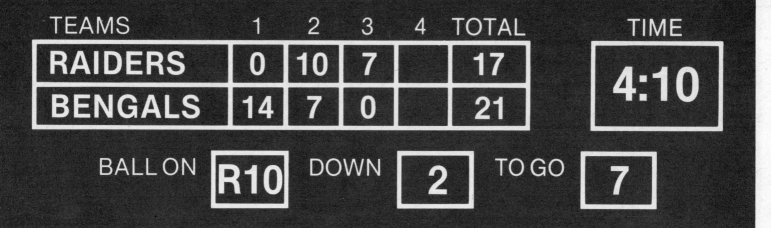

TEAMS	1	2	3	4	TOTAL
RAIDERS	0	10	7		17
BENGALS	14	7	0		21

TIME **4:10**

BALL ON **R10**   DOWN **2**   TO GO **7**

THE SITUATION In a battle of unbeatens, the game is everything one would expect from teams of this caliber. Ken Anderson, the Cincinnati Bengals' quarterback, has his team down on the Raiders' 10 looking for some insurance points. Anderson has a roster filled with good receivers: Cris Collinsworth, Issac Curtis, and his tight end, Dan Ross. He also has a powerful fullback for tough-yardage situations in Pete Johnson. Next to Johnson, Anderson himself, especially on the scramble, may be the next best runner on the team, though Charles Alexander and Archie Griffin are adequate. Someone on this squad has got to score, because there is a lot of time left. Who gets the call?

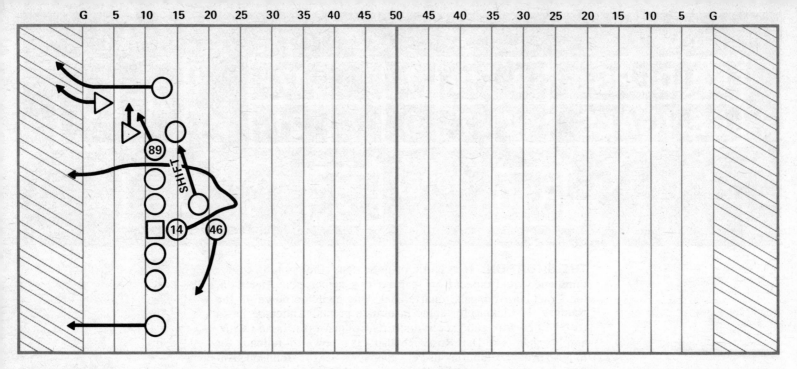

THE DECISION Ken Anderson (14) drops back slightly to the right, where he can view his receivers, most of whom are headed for the end zone. It leaves him with the option to run, too.

THE RESULT Anderson did have to run, and helped by Dan Ross (89), who was diluting the right side of the line by taking a linebacker with him, the field was open for Anderson to sneak through for the touchdown. That gave the Bengals a safe lead, and they won the game, 31–17.

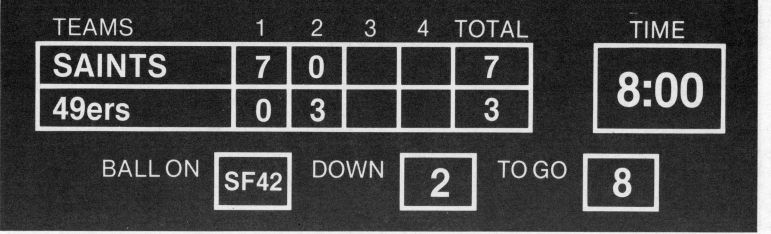

TEAMS	1	2	3	4	TOTAL
SAINTS	7	0			7
49ers	0	3			3

TIME 8:00

BALL ON SF42 DOWN 2 TO GO 8

THE SITUATION Two struggling teams—New Orleans, a perennial loser, and San Francisco, trying to recapture its Super Bowl momentum—are battling it out. New Orleans's biggest weapon, George Rogers, is admittedly overweight and was running a temperature the night before. He suffered a shoulder bruise in the first quarter. But he is back in the game. Ken Stabler is the Saints' aging quarterback. Two of the top receivers, Lindsay Scott and Kenny Duckett, are rookies, as are two of the starting guards. But the Saints hold a 7–3 lead. What is the call under these circumstances?

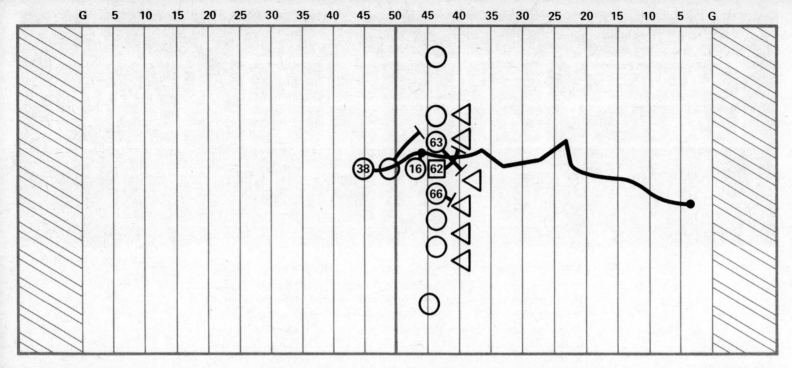

THE DECISION A handoff from Ken Stabler (16) to the meal ticket, George Rogers (38), who is the deep back in the I-formation. The young linemen up front—Brad Edelman (63) and Louis Oubre (66)—have to do their jobs, teaming with the center, John Hill (62).

THE RESULT Rogers, through his pure strength, bulled his way through the line, broke a couple of tackles, and gained 38 yards to set up the Saints' second touchdown. Rogers gained 97 yards in this game, but the 49ers salvaged the victory, 23–20.

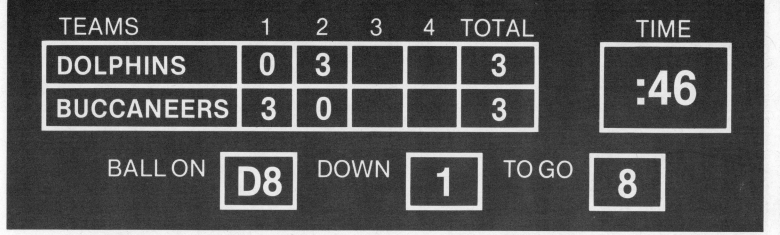

TEAMS	1	2	3	4	TOTAL	TIME
DOLPHINS	0	3			3	:46
BUCCANEERS	3	0			3	

BALL ON **D8**   DOWN **1**   TO GO **8**

THE SITUATION   Tampa Bay, in its in-state rivalry with Miami, is finally making some headway in this slow, plodding game. James Owens, the Buccaneers' running back, has carried seven straight times to the Miami 8-yard line. He has 11 carries for the game. Quarterback Doug Williams has a fine tight end, Jimmie Giles, who seems perfect for a situation this close to the goal line. But Gordon Jones, his best wide receiver, can maneuver, too. What is your call? Keep an eye on the clock.

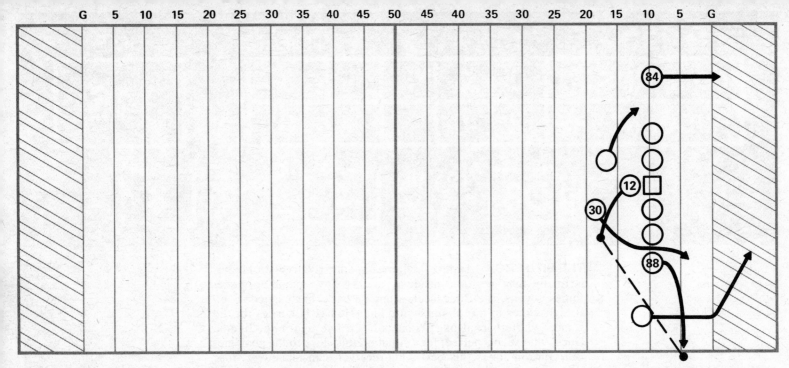

THE DECISION   James Owen (30) stayed in the game, but the play selected was a pass from Doug Williams (12) to Jimmie Giles (88). The tight end headed straight for the sideline and not even close to deep for the first touchdown of the game.

THE RESULT   Giles picked up 3 yards on this play, and Tampa Bay later settled for a field goal. But the Buccaneers did open up in the second half and upset Miami, 23–17.

OFFICIAL
TIME-
OUT!
CAPTAINS

A sign of a good football team is leadership off and on the field. The coach has the responsibility off the field, of course, but professional football teams also have captains for on the field, appointed by the coach.

Most teams have a captain for the offense, one for the defense, and another for the special teams. Many teams have two or sometimes even three captains for these units.

The captains represent a varied list of positions, as the accompanying list indicates. The roster of 1982 NFL captains was compiled early in the season, and one should note that the turnover is high (almost 50 percent) from season to season.

NFC CAPTAINS

Team	Offense	Defense	Special Teams
ATLANTA	Jeff Van Note, C Steve Bartkowski, QB	Fulton Kuykendall, LB Buddy Curry, LB	Bob Glazebrook, S
CHICAGO	All selected on game-to-game basis.		
DALLAS	Tony Dorsett, RB Pat Donovan, T	Randy White, T Dennis Thurman, CB	Ron Fellows, CB
DETROIT	Keith Dorney, T	Garry Cobb, LB	Ken Callicutt, RB
GREEN BAY	Larry McCarren, C	Johnnie Gray, S Mike Douglass, LB	Game-to-game basis.
L.A. RAMS	Cullen Bryant, RB Dennis Harrah, G	Jack Youngblood, E Cody Jones, T	Ivory Sully, S
MINNESOTA	Tommy Kramer, QB Ahmad Rashad, WR	Matt Blair, LB	
NEW ORLEANS	All selected on game-to-game basis.		
N.Y. GIANTS	Gordon King, T	George Martin, E	Frank Marion, LB Joe McLaughlin, LB
PHILADELPHIA	Guy Morriss, C	Carl Hairston, E	Louie Giammona, RB
ST. LOUIS	Dan Dierdorf, C Wayne Morris, RB Ottis Anderson, RB	Lee Nelson, S Curtis Greer, E	Game-to-game basis.
SAN FRANCISCO	All selected on game-to-game basis.		
TAMPA BAY	Steve Wilson, C Doug Williams, QB	Lee Roy Selmon, E	Cecil Johnson, LB
WASHINGTON	All selected on game-to-game basis.		

AFC CAPTAINS

Team	Offense	Defense	Special Teams
BALTIMORE	All selected on game-to-game basis.		
BUFFALO	Joe Ferguson, QB (In addition, Reggie McKenzie, G, is overall captain.)	Ben Williams, E	Phil Villapiano, LB
CINCINNATI	Archie Griffin, RB	Jim LeClair, LB	Tom Dinkel, LB
CLEVELAND	Doug Dieken, T	Dick Ambrose, LB Ron Bolton, CB	Bill Cowher, LB
DENVER	Steve Watson, WR Claudie Minor, T	Randy Gradishar, LB Tom Jackson, LB	Jim Ryan, LB Mike Harden, S
HOUSTON	Earl Campbell, RB Gifford Nielsen, QB	Robert Brazile, LB Elvin Bethea, E	Carl Roaches, KR Ted Thompson, LB
KANSAS CITY	Jack Rudnay, C Matt Herkenhoff, T	Gary Barbaro, S Gary Green, CB	Ed Beckman, TE
L.A. RAIDERS	Dave Dalby, C	Ted Hendricks, LB	Derrick Jensen, TE
MIAMI	Bob Kuechenberg, G	Earnie Rhone, LB	
NEW ENGLAND	All selected on game-to-game basis.		
N.Y. JETS	Joe Fields, C Marvin Powell, T	Joe Klecko, E Darrol Ray, S	
PITTSBURGH	Mike Webster, C	Jack Lambert, LB	
SAN DIEGO	Doug Wilkerson, G	Woodrow Lowe, LB	
SEATTLE	Steve Largent, WR	Keith Simpson, CB	Don Dufek, S

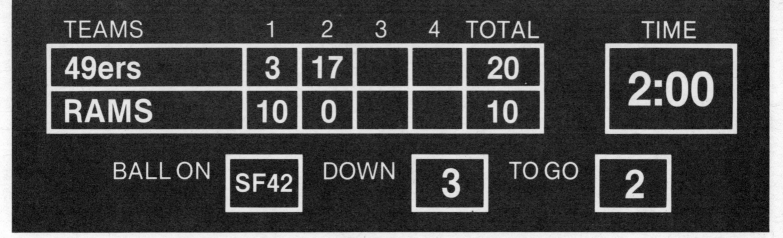

TEAMS	1	2	3	4	TOTAL	TIME
49ers	3	17			20	2:00
RAMS	10	0			10	

BALL ON **SF42** DOWN **3** TO GO **2**

THE SITUATION The Los Angeles Rams, a good scoring team with a porous defense, are on the move against the San Francisco 49ers and have decent field position as they try to get back in the game. The Rams have problems at quarterback—with Vince Ferragamo currently holding the job—and the receivers are not that prominent. The best offensive threat, at least in terms of consistency, is Wendell Tyler, the running back. A third-and-2 situation should not present too much difficulty against a San Francisco defense that has given up at least 20 points a game. Right?

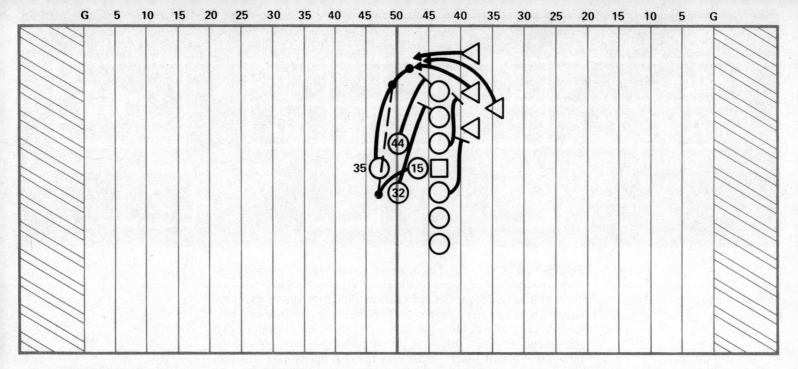

THE DECISION   Vince Ferragamo (15) lined up with a fullhouse backfield—Robert Alexander (35) at the fullback and Mike Guman (44) and Cullen Bryant (32) at the halfbacks. The call, a strange one, was for a screen pass to Alexander, picking up the blocks of Guman and Bryant.

THE RESULT   The 49ers flooded the area and swarmed Alexander for a 6-yard loss. The Rams didn't fare much better for the rest of the game, either, and lost, 30–24.

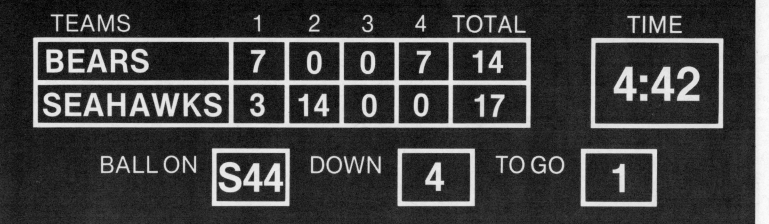

TEAMS	1	2	3	4	TOTAL
BEARS	7	0	0	7	14
SEAHAWKS	3	14	0	0	17

TIME 4:42

BALL ON **S44**　DOWN **4**　TO GO **1**

THE SITUATION The Seahawks, at midfield and protecting a lead of 3 points, went into a regular offensive lineup rather than bring in the punting team. With Jim Zorn as a quarterback, Steve Largent the wide receiver split right as a flankerback, and two regular running backs—Sherman Smith and Dan Doornink—in the backfield, there were many play options to get the first down. By going for it, the Seahawks supposedly could hold the ball and run down the clock. But not punting was a risky choice, too.

Still, the Seahawks prepared to go for the first down and keep their playoff hopes alive. What type of play would you call to get you out of a tough spot?

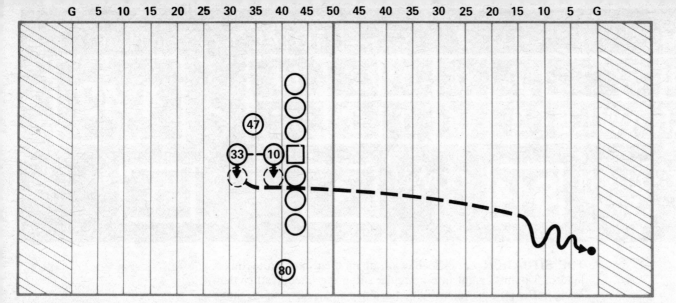

THE DECISION Follow carefully: the Seahawks decided to punt, but not before some shenanigins. Jim Zorn (10) was at quarterback, Dan Doornink (33) at fullback, and Sherman Smith (47) at halfback. But Zorn, without bending over the ball, turned to say something to Smith. Then, he turned right and began barking signals to Steve Largent (80), his wide receiver way to the right. Doornink, in the meantime, was standing at fullback, playing the waiting game. The ball was then snapped directly to Doornink while Zorn was still shouting, and Doornink took a step to his right and punted the ball.

THE RESULT The opposing coach, Mike Ditka, later called it a "high school play," but it worked. Doornink, who had quick-kicked a couple of times at Washington State, boomed the ball 54 yards. The Bears' linemen, kneeling to wait till Zorn got his signals straight, were caught completely off guard. Seattle later stopped the Bears and added another field goal to win, 20–14.

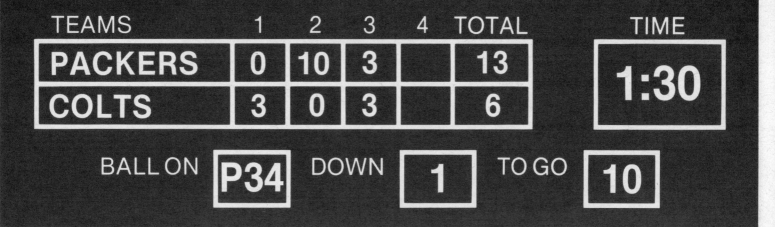

TEAMS	1	2	3	4	TOTAL
PACKERS	0	10	3		13
COLTS	3	0	3		6

TIME 1:30

BALL ON **P34** DOWN **1** TO GO **10**

THE SITUATION   The Baltimore Colts have not won a game in their first five of the season. But they also have not been playing that badly. Again, they were hanging in, late in the game, against a pretty good Green Bay team.

Thus, the Packers ought to get on the scoreboard at least one more time to feel safe. But the Packers' offense, with all its awesome potential and receivers like John Jefferson and James Lofton, has been dragging for the second game in a row.

Anyway, it's first down back in your own territory and you have to get your team moving. What do you call?

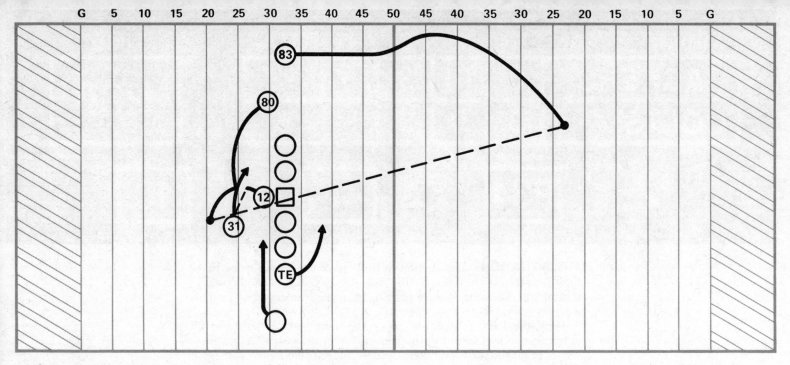

THE DECISION The Packers came up with a beauty. James Lofton (80), in the slot to the left, was a high school quarterback. Some people have called him the best "pure" athlete in the NFL. The play calls for Lynn Dickey (12) to take a couple of steps back out of his quarterback position and pitch the ball to Gerry Ellis (31) swinging left. But Ellis turns to Lofton coming around and gives him a handoff on a reverse. But that is not all. Lofton fakes a run with a couple of steps, then drops back and throws a long one to John Jefferson (83), who has had all this time to get far downfield.

THE RESULT Jefferson caught the ball, good for 43 yards and a first down, and the Packers went on to score. But the Colts got over the stunning play and managed to tie the Packers, 20–20, before the day was over.

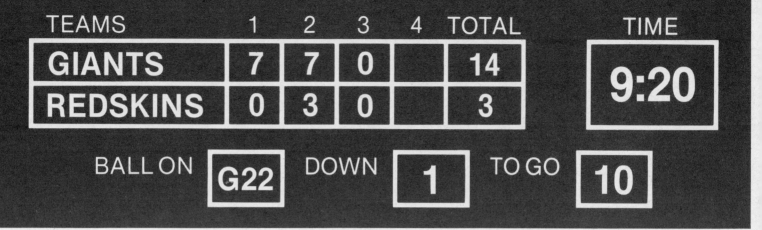

TEAMS	1	2	3	4	TOTAL	TIME
GIANTS	7	7	0		14	9:20
REDSKINS	0	3	0		3	

BALL ON **G22** DOWN **1** TO GO **10**

THE SITUATION On a nasty, wet, snowy day in Washington, the New York Giants are sitting with a good lead but being threatened by the Redskins. Joe Theismann's pass to Charlie Brown gave them a first down. Theismann has been effective and has passed often in the bad weather, but only for about 10 yards per completion. John Riggins has been doing almost all of the rushing among the deep backs, but Theismann has been forced into some runs by the Giant defense. The Redskins need a touchdown because it is difficult to say how bad the weather will get. They are in good field position, so what should they do?

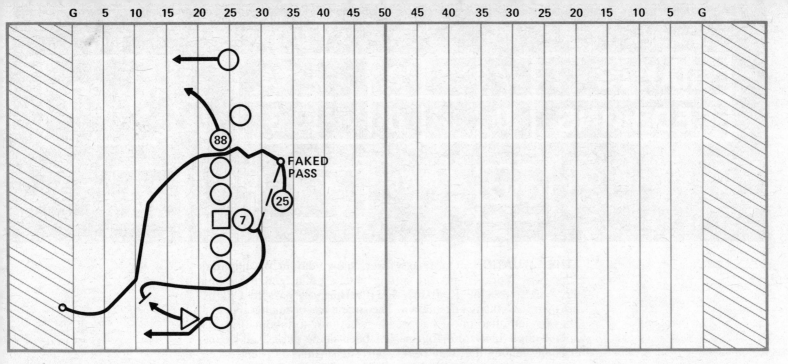

FAKED
PASS

THE DECISION The Redskins have Joe Washington (25) in the game for John Riggins. Rick Walker (88) is the tight end. The call is for Joe Theismann (7) to shovel a lateral to Washington, sweeping left, then for Washington to pass, possibly to Walker.

THE RESULT A broken play that broke the Giants. Washington got ready to pass, couldn't find his man, zigzagged through the line, and took off to the left side of the field, weaving his way for some big yardage. He was about 10 yards from the goal line when he picked up an outstanding block by Theismann that sprung him loose to score. The Redskins went on to win this game, 15–14.

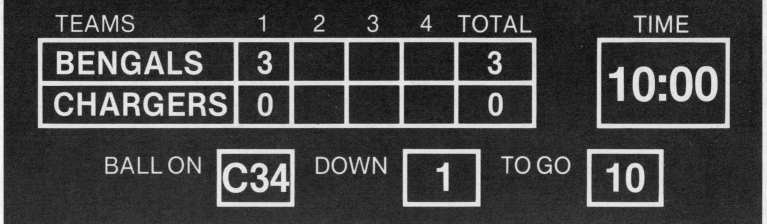

TEAMS	1	2	3	4	TOTAL	TIME
BENGALS	3				3	10:00
CHARGERS	0				0	

BALL ON **C34** DOWN **1** TO GO **10**

THE SITUATION   This is the first of six plays from one of the best, if not the most exciting, regular-season games of 1982, between San Diego and Cincinnati. It took place on a Monday night in San Diego.

The Chargers are behind by a field goal, but it is early, and they are getting ready to mount a drive behind Dan Fouts, the strong-armed quarterback. With his many talented receivers and a pair of outstanding running backs in Chuck Muncie and James Brooks, he has an arsenal like no one in professional football. How do you use those weapons on this play?

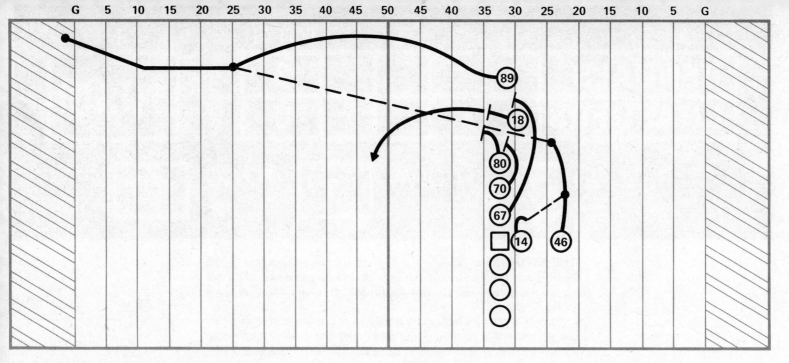

THE DECISION Dan Fouts (14) takes a couple of steps back to pass and then pitches the lateral to Chuck Muncie (46), the single running back. Ed White (67) and Russ Washington (70) pull to lead the blocking for what seems to be a sweep. Kellen Winslow (80) has already pulled away and to the right of the scrimmage line to block. Wes Chandler (89) has dashed downfield on an ordinary fly pattern. Charlie Joiner (18) has gone downfield, but short. But it is a Muncie pass, not a sweep, and the target is Chandler.

THE RESULT A 66-yard touchdown pass that Chandler caught on the 25 and carried in. (Another play from this game follows.)

TEAMS	1	2	3	4	TOTAL	TIME
BENGALS	3				3	5:00
CHARGERS	7				7	

BALL ON **C39** DOWN **2** TO GO **3**

THE SITUATION Cincinnati has the ball and is on the move. With Pete Johnson at fullback and Ken Anderson, a good runner, at quarterback, the Bengals could attack on the ground. Isaac Curtis is a good long threat, Cris Collinsworth is excellent coming across the middle, and Dan Ross, the tight end, can handle the short passes, as well as others. What do you call?

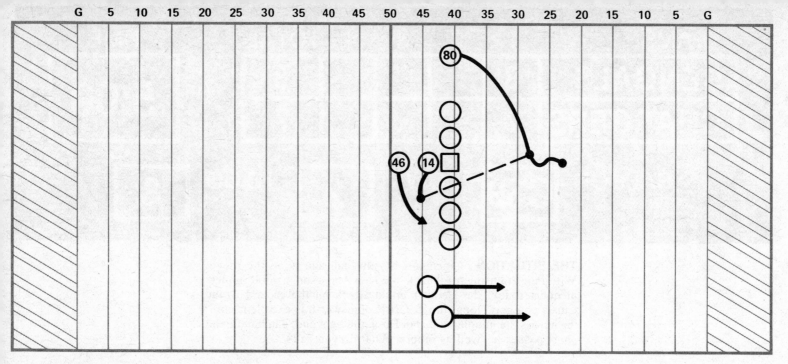

THE DECISION The target is Cris Collinsworth (80) over the middle. Nothing special about the play, with Pete Johnson (46) sweeping right and Ken Anderson (14) rolling out just a bit before making the quick pass.

THE RESULT Collinsworth made the catch on the fly at the 28-yard line and gained 5 more for a total of 16 yards and a first down. The Bengals went on to score their first touchdown of the game. (Another play from this game follows.)

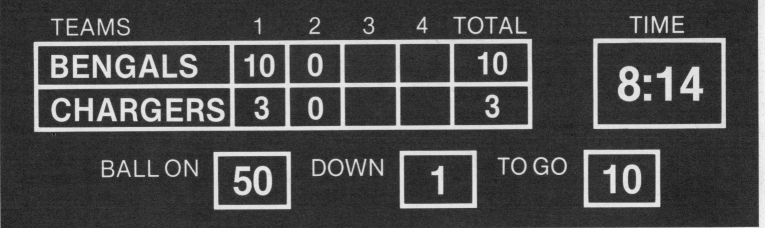

TEAMS	1	2	3	4	TOTAL	TIME
BENGALS	10	0			10	8:14
CHARGERS	3	0			3	

BALL ON **50**   DOWN **1**   TO GO **10**

THE SITUATION   San Diego has yet to get its first touchdown and is struggling at midfield. The Chargers have a first down, with all the usual options, but something long or medium long would seem desirable. What do you think?

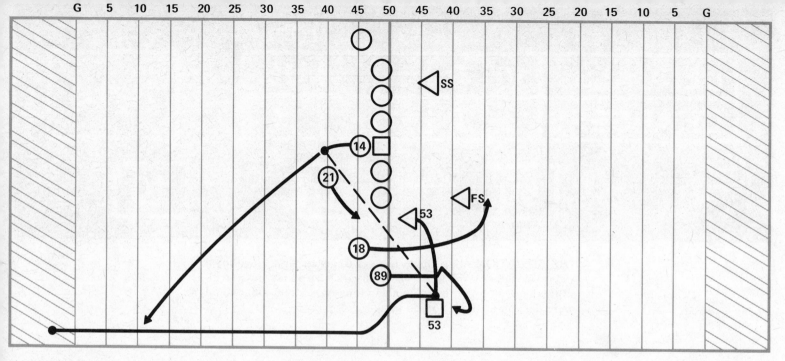

THE DECISION   Dan Fouts (14) has the right side loaded with Wes Chandler (89) and Charlie Joiner (18) to beat the zone defense. James Brooks (21) is his only back. The call is for Chandler to put on some moves and hook over near the right sideline for about a 15-yarder.

THE RESULT   The Bengals' Bo Harris (53) was waiting as Chandler was making all his squiggly moves, and by the time Chandler made his final turn, Harris had the interception and an open lane to the goal line. Fouts had a shot at the linebacker but only made a feeble attempt to tackle him. Harris was credited with a 62-yard return. (Another play from this game follows.)

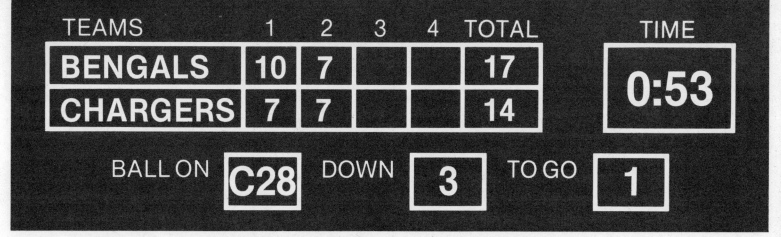

TEAMS	1	2	3	4	TOTAL	TIME
BENGALS	10	7			17	0:53
CHARGERS	7	7			14	

BALL ON **C28** DOWN **3** TO GO **1**

THE SITUATION The game is becoming wide open, and the Bengals are roaring downfield again. But time is running out in the half. Anderson has already thrown the ball 32 times and completed 24. But it is third down and 1, and he has Pete Johnson, the 250-pounder, at fullback if he wants to use him. What is the call?

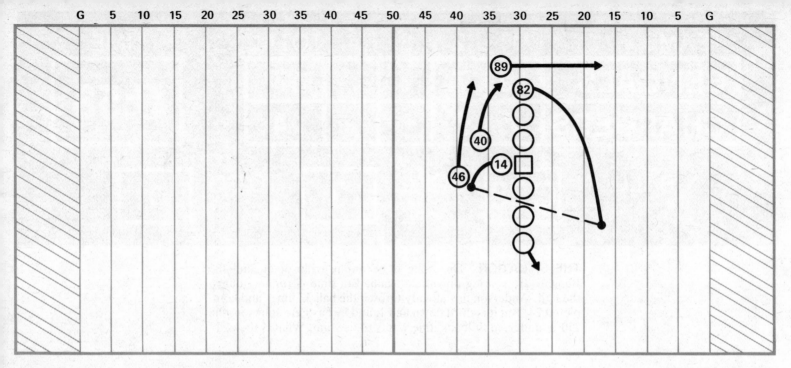

THE DECISION   The Bengals, with Ken Anderson (14) at quarterback, go with two tight ends, including the rookie, Rodney Holman (82). Another tight end, Dan Ross (89), is playing off Holman's outside shoulder. Charles Alexander (40) joins Pete Johnson (46) in the backfield. Anderson's play is to hit Holman coming across the middle after hoping that the Chargers expect the run.

THE RESULT   Holman came well across the middle to shake his man and get the ball—a good play that gained 10 yards and put the Bengals in position to add a field goal before the half. (Another play from this game follows.)

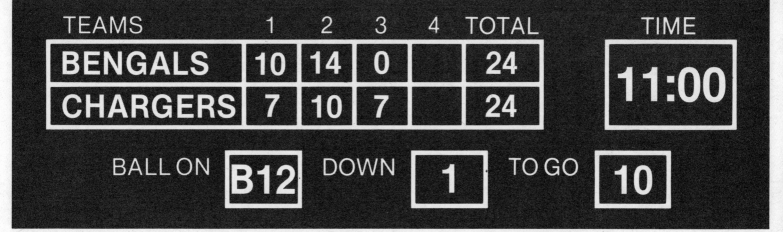

TEAMS	1	2	3	4	TOTAL	TIME
BENGALS	10	14	0		24	**11:00**
CHARGERS	7	10	7		24	

BALL ON **B12**　DOWN **1**　TO GO **10**

THE SITUATION The game is tied, but Cincinnati has its back to the wall. However, a marksman like Ken Anderson can pass out of this situation. Would you let him if you were the coach?

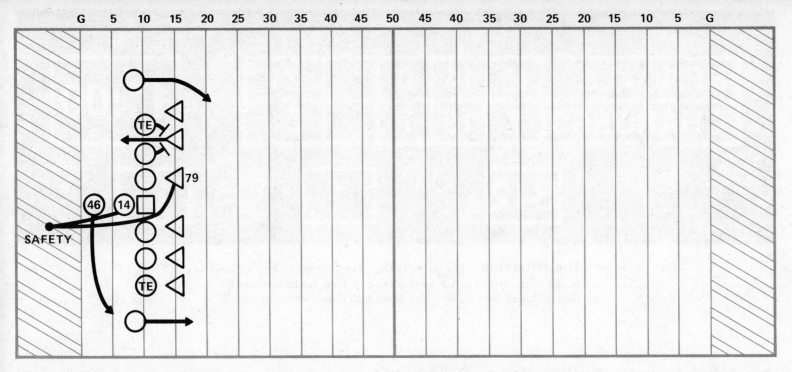

THE DECISION Ken Anderson (14) does set up for the pass, with two tight ends in the game and both receivers set very wide. Pete Johnson (46) is the lone deep back. Anderson has lots of targets to look for, including Johnson, who flares out to the right.

THE RESULT Anderson dropped well into the end zone to pass, but Gary Johnson (79), the Chargers' right tackle, looped around the line and into the end zone to nail Anderson for a safety. (Another play from this game follows.)

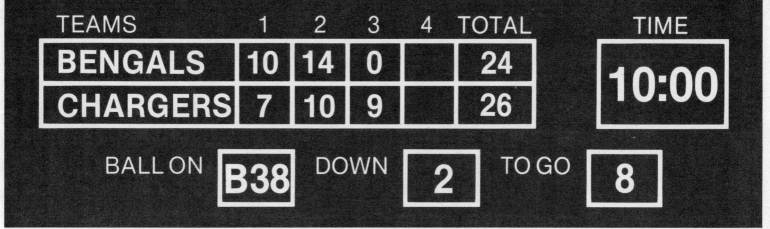

TEAMS	1	2	3	4	TOTAL	TIME
BENGALS	10	14	0		24	10:00
CHARGERS	7	10	9		26	

BALL ON **B38**   DOWN **2**   TO GO **8**

THE SITUATION Chargers' ball and they, like the Bengals, are passing like crazy in this game. Ken Anderson will end the night with 56 passes, Dan Fouts with 40, plus the Chuck Muncie touchdown throw. Between the two teams, almost 900 yards in completions will be registered. But San Diego is showing a fine rushing game, too. The Chargers are nursing a 2-point lead and know they must score more before the night is over. How do they go about it on this play?

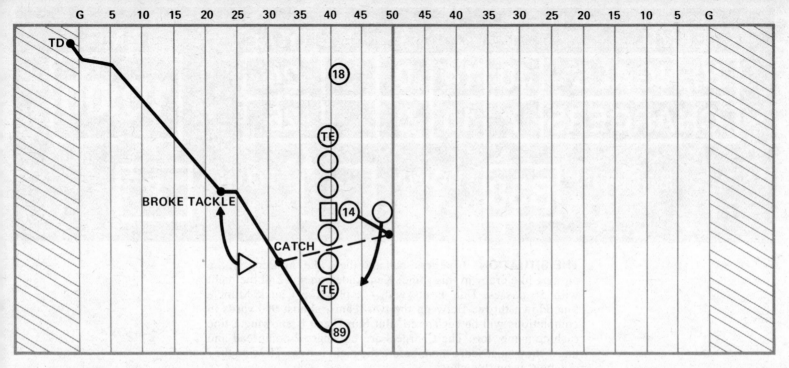

THE DECISION   A pass from Dan Fouts (14) to Wes Chandler (89) breaking over the middle. This is a two-tight-end setup, and Charlie Joiner (18) is split wide to the right.

THE RESULT   Chandler made the catch at the Cincinnati 31 and broke a tackle about 8 yards down the field. From there, he went in for the touchdown in a wild third quarter that saw both teams score a combined total of 33 points. The Chargers never fell behind in the game and eventually won, 50–34.

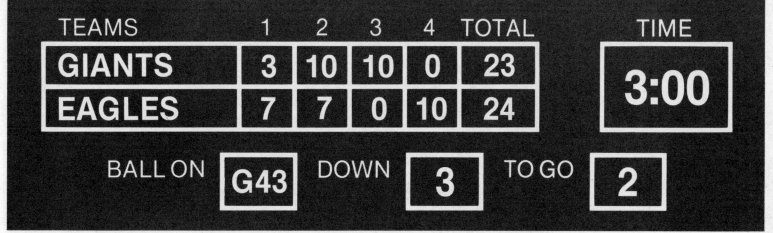

TEAMS	1	2	3	4	TOTAL
GIANTS	3	10	10	0	23
EAGLES	7	7	0	10	24

TIME **3:00**

BALL ON **G43** DOWN **3** TO GO **2**

THE SITUATION The Giants are driving on the Eagles late in the game and are confronted with a third-down situation. But in this game, the New Yorkers have made more than half of their tries on third down. This Giant possession began on the New York 35, and the Giants picked up 8 yards on carries by Rob Carpenter and Butch Woolfolk. Several other times when the Giants converted on third down, it was on passes by Scott Brunner. How do you keep up the success rate and keep plugging away to get the go-ahead score?

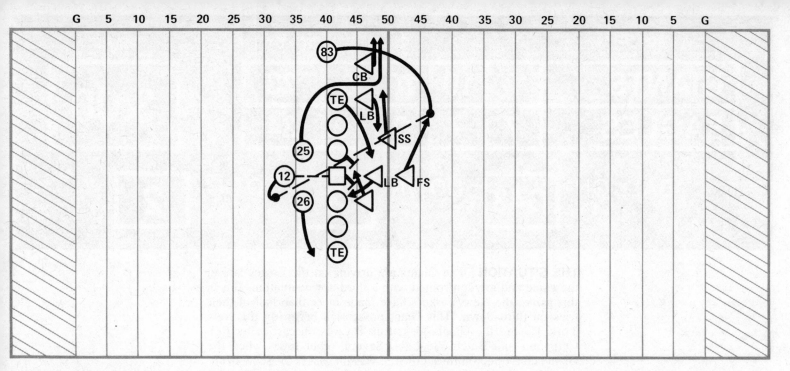

THE DECISION The Giants went into a shotgun, with Scott Brunner (12) flanked by Butch Woolfolk (25) and Rob Carpenter (26). Earnest Gray (83) is split to the left. Woolfolk's job is to circle around the right side and cut upfield and then to the sideline. Gray comes out from behind Woolfolk and cuts in toward the middle, hoping to confuse the safety and the cornerback, who are covering him and Woolfolk.

THE RESULT Gray shook free of the cornerback on his shoulder as the cornerback switched to Woolfolk. Gray made the catch, good for 14 yards. From there, the Giants gained another 35 yards on five plays and set themselves in position for the winning field goal, which made the final score, 26–24.

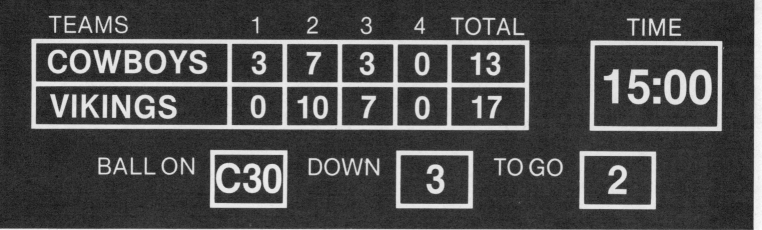

TEAMS	1	2	3	4	TOTAL
COWBOYS	3	7	3	0	13
VIKINGS	0	10	7	0	17

TIME **15:00**

BALL ON **C30**   DOWN **3**   TO GO **2**

THE SITUATION   In the final game of the regular season, the Vikings need a victory to get to the playoffs. After three quarters, they are playing a solid game both offensively and defensively and hold a slim lead. Now, on the first play of the final quarter, the Cowboys are trying to come back. It is short yardage on third down, and you've got the runners, like Tony Dorsett and Ron Springs, and you've got the short receivers, like Doug Cosbie, the tight end. And if you want to go for the big one, Drew Pearson and Tony Hill can break a game open. What is your choice of play?

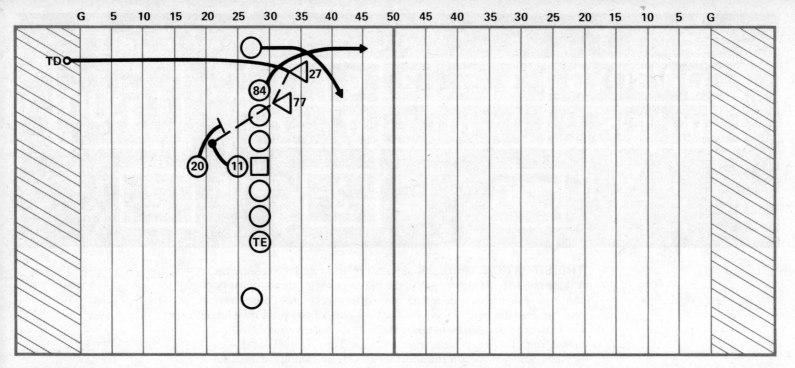

THE DECISION The Cowboys decide to play it somewhat safe and go to Doug Cosbie (84), one of two tight ends in the game. Danny White (11) has only one deep back, Ron Springs (20). Cosbie crisscrosses with the wide receiver to the right and heads for the sideline not too far away. White gives the little fake to Springs and throws quickly.

THE RESULT Mark Mullaney (77), a Minnesota tackle, stepped into the passing lane and deflected the ball. John Turner (27) picked it off as Cosbie was behind him. Turner scampered 33 yards for the touchdown. (Another play from this game follows.)

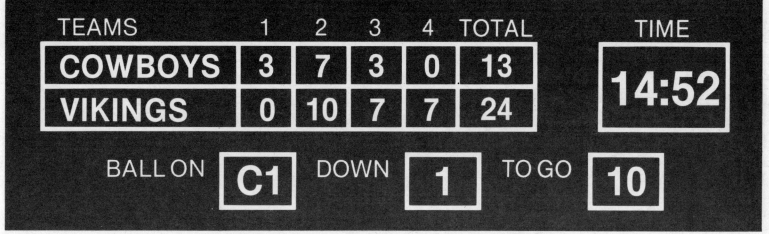

TEAMS	1	2	3	4	TOTAL
COWBOYS	3	7	3	0	13
VIKINGS	0	10	7	7	24

TIME **14:52**

BALL ON **C1** DOWN **1** TO GO **10**

THE SITUATION The Cowboys have problems. After the Vikings' previous touchdown, the Cowboys mishandle the kickoff and are stuck with the ball on their own 1-yard line. Actually, it's more like the 1-foot line. There is still time to get back into the game, but 99 2/3 yards is quite a distance. At this time, it is a case of survival. You've got some tough backs like Tony Dorsett, Ron Springs, and Robert Newhouse, who can get you some breathing room, or even Danny White on a keeper from quarterback. Or do you go short to the tight ends? You name it.

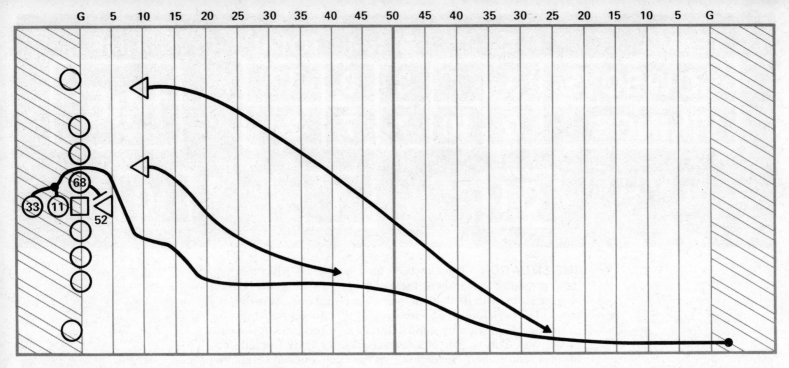

THE DECISION   Let Tony Dorsett (33) go up the middle and try to get the breathing room. A safety, a fumble, or an interception would really put the Cowboys in a bind, and Dorsett is strong enough to bull his way for a couple of yards. The Cowboys set up with Danny White (11) over the center and use two tight ends and two wide receivers.

THE RESULT   NFL history, as Dorsett went over right guard, picked up a great block by Herbert Scott (68) on Ray Preston (52), and broke loose to go all the way. The 99-yard run from scrimmage set an NFL record. It also got Dallas back in the game. (Another play from this game follows.)

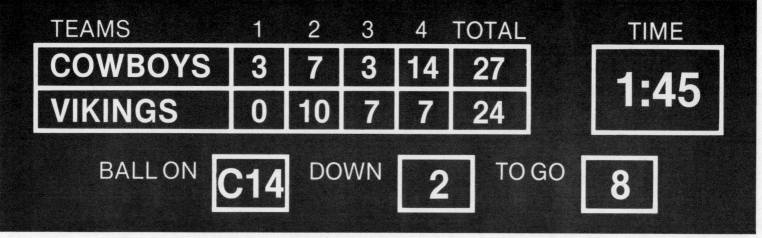

TEAMS	1	2	3	4	TOTAL	TIME
COWBOYS	3	7	3	14	27	1:45
VIKINGS	0	10	7	7	24	

BALL ON **C14** DOWN **2** TO GO **8**

THE SITUATION The Cowboys, sparked by Tony Dorsett's run and a 64-yard touchdown drive, are back in the lead, and time is running out on the Vikings, who must win to make the playoffs. But the Vikings have marched 66 yards on 10 plays, mostly passes by Tommy Kramer, who is having a fairly good game. Ted Brown has 100 yards rushing and another 50 on pass receptions. Kramer has thrown to nine different receivers even though he has only 17 completions. Terry LeCount is the only one besides Brown, however, who has caught more than two. Keep in mind you might want to play it safe here and protect your field position for a field goal. With almost 2 minutes left, however, the thought has to be touchdown so that Dallas cannot come back and score its own field goal. How do you get it?

77

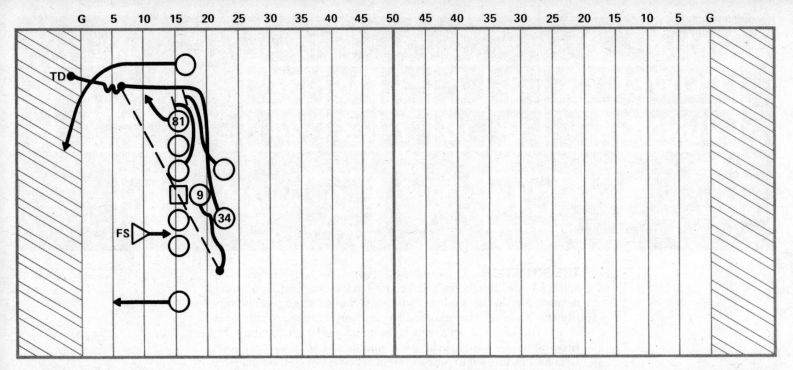

THE DECISION Ted Brown is out of the game, replaced in the backfield by Rickey Young (34). Joe Senser (81) is at tight end. The play is for a pass to Young coming out of the backfield. The wide receivers go into the end zone, giving Young some room to catch between the 5- and 10-yard lines. Tommy Kramer (9) first fakes to Young, then can roll out and try to hit one of the other receivers.

THE RESULT Young made the move around right end after the fake and continued downfield. Kramer looked left, drawing the attention away from Young, then turned right and hit him on the 6-yard line. Young fell to the 5 but got up and scored what turned out to be the winning touchdown in a 31–27 game.

SECOND QUARTER
THE SUPER BOWL TOURNAMENT

2ND QUARTER

For the first time in its 63 seasons, the NFL allowed 16 teams into its playoffs, dubbing the postseason extravaganza "the Super Bowl Tournament."

It was not until the final Monday night game of the season, when Minnesota upset Dallas, that the final pairings were set. Teams such as Detroit of the National Football Conference (NFC) and Cleveland of the American Football Conference (AFC) made the playoffs with 4–5–0 marks; the San Francisco 49ers, the defending Super Bowl champions, did not. The extra game in the playoffs did a lot toward adding a new dimension to the strategies used. As it turned out, both strong and weak teams in the playoffs had to exercise extra imagination in the form of plays to survive.

Through eight quarterfinal games and four semifinal games, most of the best teams survived indeed, but not without the struggle and imagination that got them that far.

Teams turned more and more to the big-play theory—the game-breakers that can make a difference.

On the following pages, which the editors consider 1982's second quarter, are some of those plays that led four teams to their respective conference championship contests.

THE TOURNAMENT

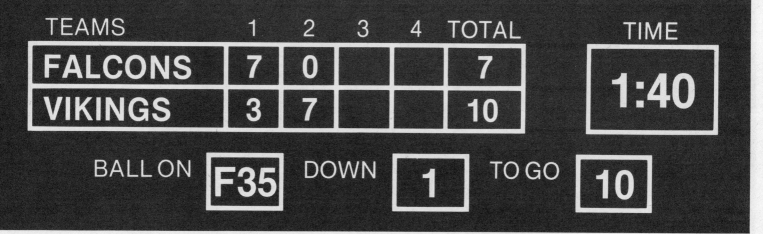

TEAMS	1	2	3	4	TOTAL
FALCONS	7	0			7
VIKINGS	3	7			10

TIME 1:40

BALL ON **F35** DOWN **1** TO GO **10**

THE SITUATION Minnesota has a drive going just before the half. Ted Brown, the Vikings' running back, is having a good day and so is Tommy Kramer, the quarterback. It is one of those situations where you can try a variety of plays, but you have to keep the clock in mind if you want to get one more score by halftime. What is your play?

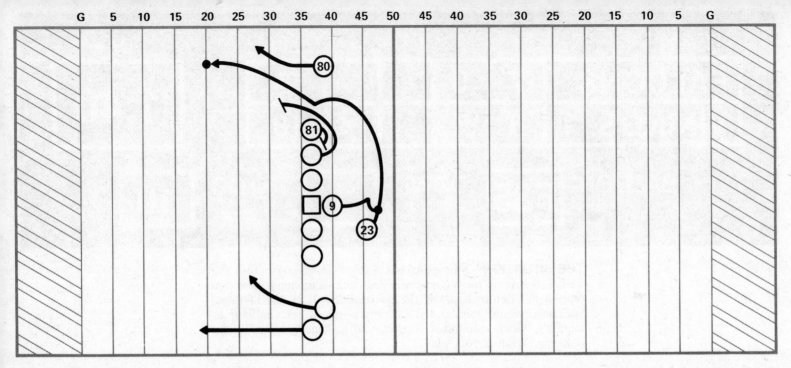

THE DECISION With just Brown (23) as the single running back, the Vikings load up with a lot of receivers for Kramer (9) to choose from. Joe Senser (81) and Terry LeCount (80) are on the strong side. But the call is for a handoff to Brown after a fake pump by Kramer.

THE RESULT Turned out to be a fine call, as Brown picked up 14 yards and another first down. It was almost a Statue of Liberty play the way Kramer held his arm up to take the pass and then quickly settled the ball into Brown's arms. The Vikings went on to get their field goal before the half. (Another play from this game follows.)

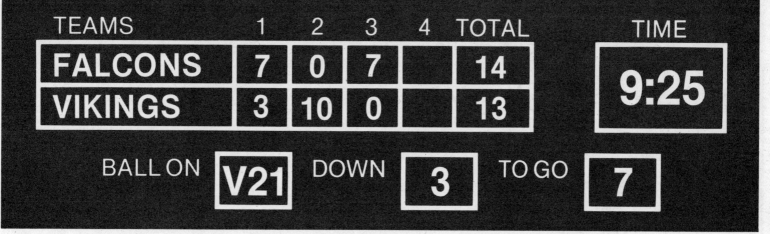

TEAMS	1	2	3	4	TOTAL	TIME
FALCONS	7	0	7		14	9:25
VIKINGS	3	10	0		13	

BALL ON **V21**   DOWN **3**   TO GO **7**

THE SITUATION   The Vikings are threatening to regain the lead from the surprising Falcons. It is an obvious passing down, but what can you come up with to make it difficult for the Falcons?

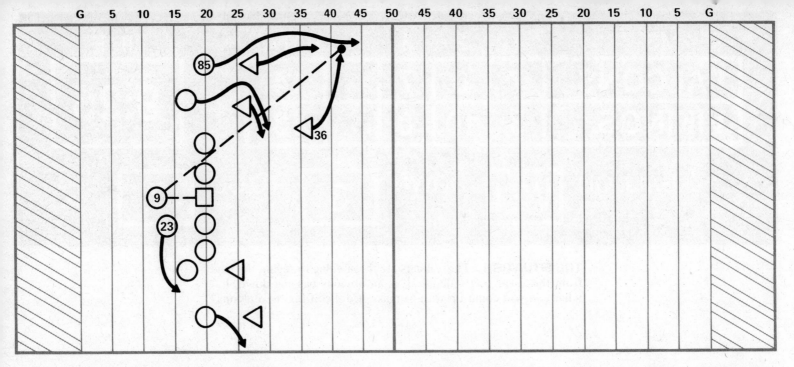

THE DECISION The Vikings put Tommy Kramer (9) into the shotgun, with Ted Brown (23) back with him. The call is for a pretty simple fly pattern to Sammy White (85), based on White's ability to spring loose and outsprint the opposition. As usual, the Vikings have a lot of receivers split wide.

THE RESULT Kramer's pass was underthrown and intercepted by a safety, Bob Glazebrook (36). (Another play from this game follows.)

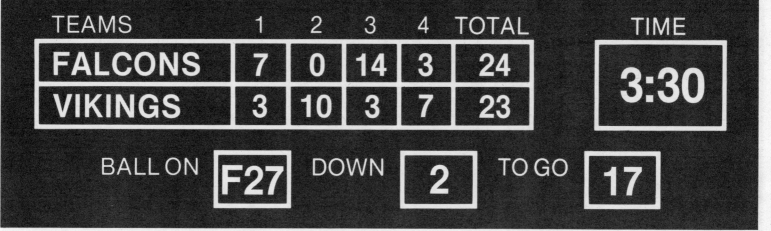

TEAMS	1	2	3	4	TOTAL
FALCONS	7	0	14	3	24
VIKINGS	3	10	3	7	23

TIME 3:30

BALL ON F27 **DOWN** 2 **TO GO** 17

THE SITUATION The problem with the first round of the so-called Super Bowl Tournament was a number of runaway games, but the Falcons and Vikings had no such problem as they battled throughout in their contest.

The Vikings find themselves in a tough spot near the end of the game, with the Falcons holding a 1-point lead. The Vikings are close to field-goal range, but not close enough to count on an easy, sure-thing kick. And who is to say a field goal is going to be enough with more than 3 minutes left on the clock?

Long yardage and not an easy decision to make. What do you call?

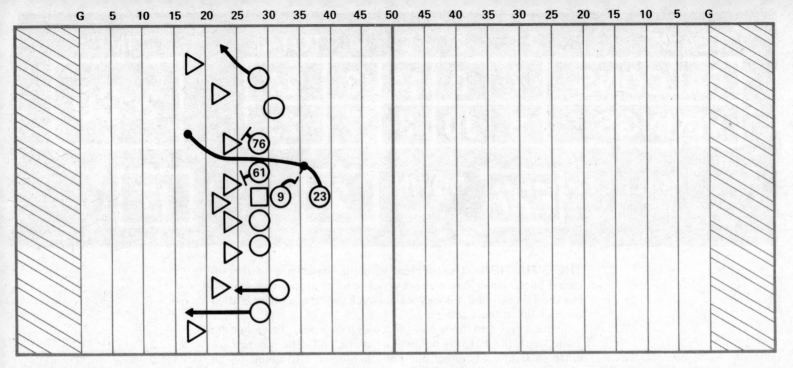

THE DECISION The Vikings line up in their wide spread formation, with Tommy Kramer (9) over the center and Ted Brown (23) the lone running back. Kramer has been throwing the ball often and well all day, so it may look to the Falcons like a passing situation. But the call is a power run off tackle by Brown, going over the strong side.

THE RESULT A 10-yard gain, due in no small part to Brown's ruggedness going through the defense. Two good blocks, by Wes Hamilton (61) and Tim Irwin (76), sprung him loose.

The Vikings went on to score a decisive touchdown to win the game, 30–24.

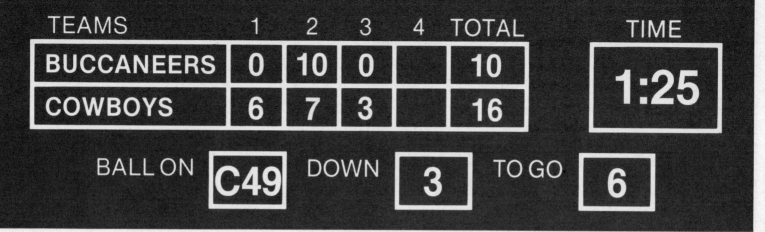

TEAMS	1	2	3	4	TOTAL
BUCCANEERS	0	10	0		10
COWBOYS	6	7	3		16

TIME 1:25

BALL ON C49 **DOWN** 3 **TO GO** 6

THE SITUATION Tampa Bay has the ball at midfield on an apparent passing down. You've got a flier in the lineup in Gordon Jones, a strong-arm thrower in Doug Williams, but also a good short-yardage tight end in Jimmie Giles. You need a touchdown, but do you get greedy and go for the bomb or peck away and get the first down?

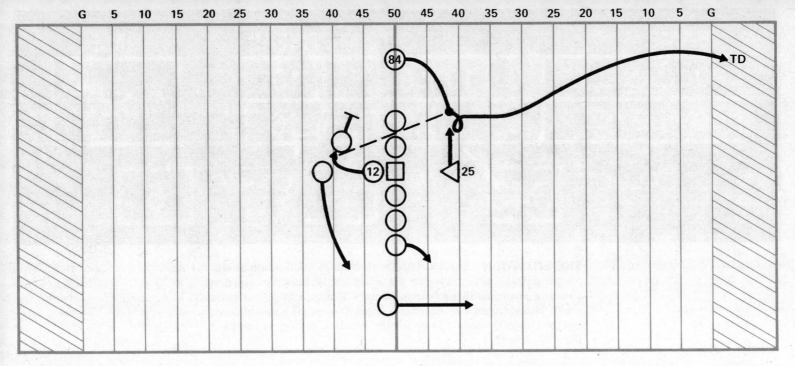

THE DECISION Williams (12) called for a first-down-length pass to Jones (84) out on the left flank. Nothing real fancy, just get the first down.

THE RESULT What the Buccaneers got was not what they expected. Jones caught the ball on the Cowboys' 42 but broke a tackle attempt by Rod Hill (25) a few yards downfield and ran away to score a touchdown. (Another play from this game follows.)

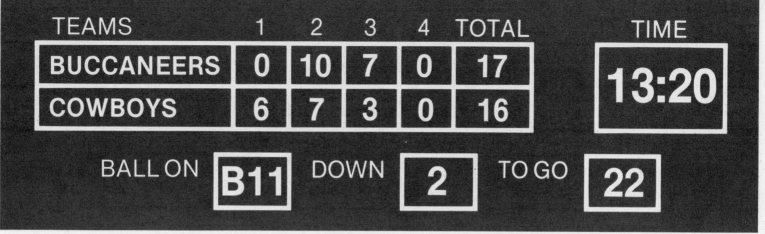

TEAMS	1	2	3	4	TOTAL
BUCCANEERS	0	10	7	0	17
COWBOYS	6	7	3	0	16

TIME
13:20

BALL ON **B11** DOWN **2** TO GO **22**

THE SITUATION   Two penalties put Tampa Bay back on its own 11-yard line with very long yardage. Not an easy play selection when you are in this kind of trouble. A pass is a must, but is dangerous. A run will do little good but buy time before a punt. You've got to do something. What?

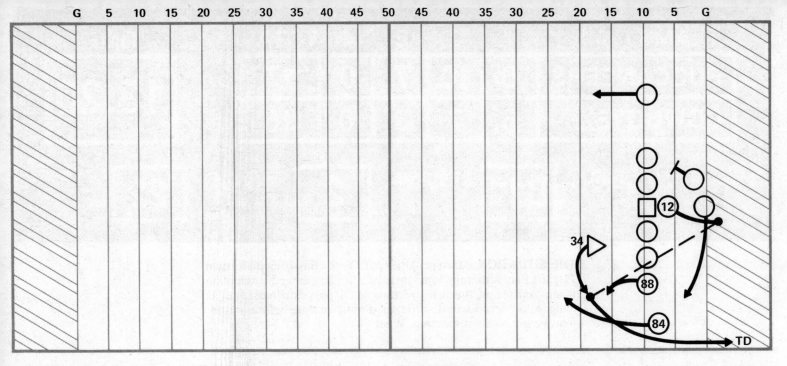

THE DECISION Let fly to Gordon Jones (84), the wide receiver.

THE RESULT A costly interception by the Cowboys' Monty Hunter (34), who came up and picked off the underthrown ball by Doug Williams (12) and returned it for a touchdown. (Another play from this game follows.)

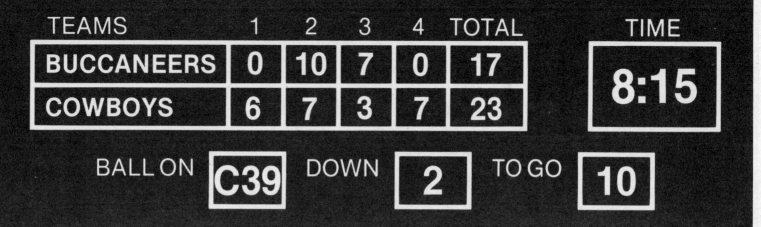

TEAMS	1	2	3	4	TOTAL
BUCCANEERS	0	10	7	0	17
COWBOYS	6	7	3	7	23

TIME 8:15

BALL ON C39 **DOWN** 2 **TO GO** 10

THE SITUATION With Dallas in the lead, the Buccaneers have yet another shot to get back into the game midway through the final period. Again, the Bucs are in a passing situation. So far, Williams has been going mostly to his wide receivers and not having much luck, making only about one-third of his attempts. The rushing game by James Wilder, particularly, has been good, but this doesn't seem like a running situation. Williams has not utilized his fine tight end, Jimmie Giles, at all. What do you do to spark the Bucs?

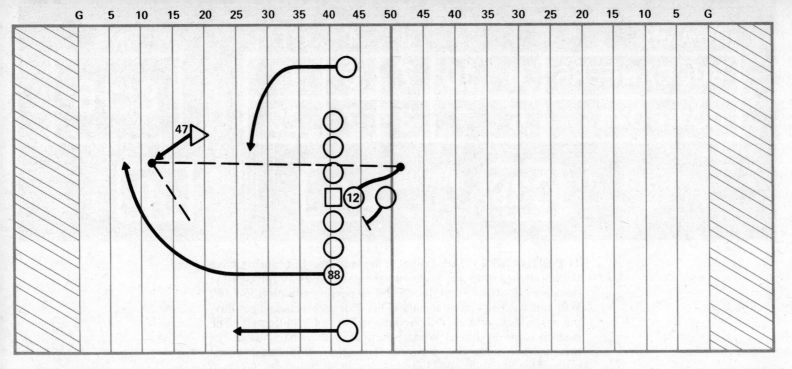

G 5 10 15 20 25 30 35 40 45 50 45 40 35 30 25 20 15 10 5 G

THE DECISION   Williams (12) finally went for Giles (88) on a long pattern.

THE RESULT   Even though Giles was little used in this game, the Cowboys were waiting for him. Dextor Clinkscale (47) knocked the ball down before it got to Giles, and the drive was thwarted.

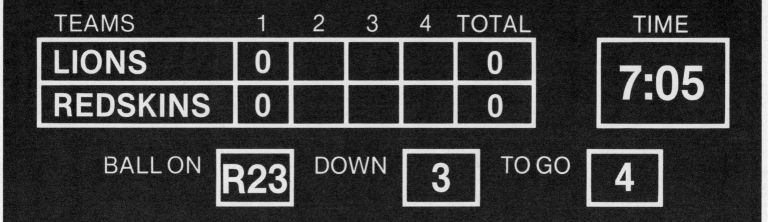

TEAMS	1	2	3	4	TOTAL	TIME
LIONS	0				0	7:05
REDSKINS	0				0	

BALL ON **R23**   DOWN **3**   TO GO **4**

THE SITUATION The Lions, who made the playoffs with a meager 4–5 record, are in need of some fast scoring if they expect to stay in the game with the Washington Redskins, who had the best record in the NFC.

The Lions moved the ball well on this drive and are not far from scoring territory. So this is a big play. What would your selection be?

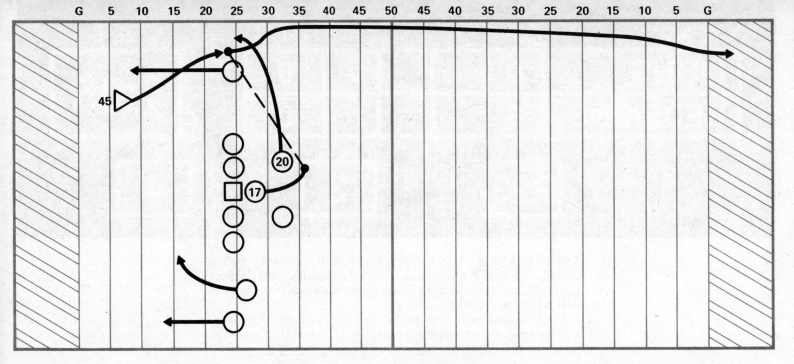

THE DECISION Eric Hipple (17) goes to Billy Sims (20) on a pass out to the flat. The main thing is to get the ball to Sims just about at the line of scrimmage and let him find some running room. It is a dangerous pass if it doesn't work because the defender has the whole field in front of him in case of an interception or a fumble.

THE RESULT The interception is what happened, as Jeris White (45) came out of the zone to pick the ball away from Sims. White returned it 77 yards for a touchdown. (Another play from this game follows.)

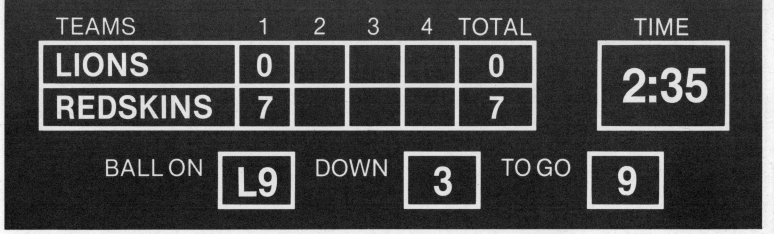

TEAMS	1	2	3	4	TOTAL	TIME
LIONS	0				0	**2:35**
REDSKINS	7				7	

BALL ON **L9** DOWN **3** TO GO **9**

THE SITUATION The Redskins have one touchdown on the board and are looking for another early in the game. But they are faced with a tough passing down.

Do they try some of their trickery? Stick to basics?

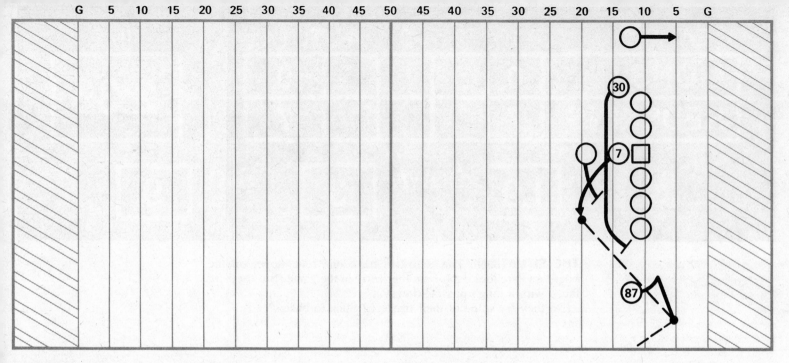

THE DECISION This is no place to get cute. The call is for a pass from Joe Theismann (7) to Charlie Brown (87), who runs to the inside, then cuts to the sideline just before the goal line. Nick Giaquinto (30) is on the move from left to right to create a little turmoil, but that is as close as this play is to being fancy.

THE RESULT Theismann almost pulled it off, but Brown dropped the ball on the 3-yard line. The Redskins had to settle for a field goal, but they went on to easily defeat the Lions, 31–7.

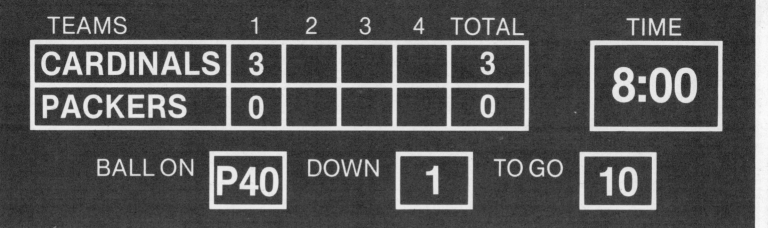

TEAMS	1	2	3	4	TOTAL	TIME
CARDINALS	3				3	**8:00**
PACKERS	0				0	

BALL ON **P40**   DOWN **1**   TO GO **10**

THE SITUATION The Packers have the great receivers, John Jefferson and James Lofton, and it is early in the game. As the saying goes, "If you got the cannons, shoot them." But with first down and the game young, the varied Packer offense can also go to its fine running back, Eddie Lee Ivery, or the strong tight end, Paul Coffman. Which cannon do you fire?

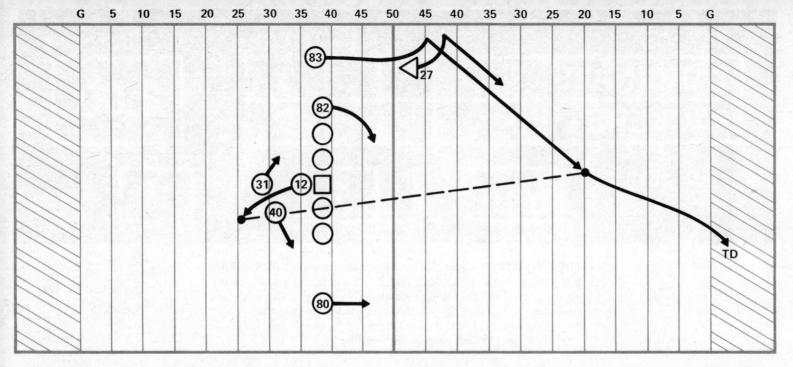

THE DECISION Long and to Jefferson (83) over on the left flank. The power is to the left, with Coffman (82) the tight end on that side, Lofton (80) is to the right, with two runners, Ivery (40) and Gerry Ellis (31) in the backfield with Lynn Dickey (12).

THE RESULT Jefferson made a great move on the Cardinals' Carl Allen (27), forcing Allen to turn his back as Jefferson turned in on a move to the goal posts. Jefferson caught the ball on the 20-yard line and had an easy jaunt to the end zone for the game's first touchdown. The Packers went on to an easy 41–16 victory. Dickey later hit Jefferson again and Lofton for touchdowns in this game.

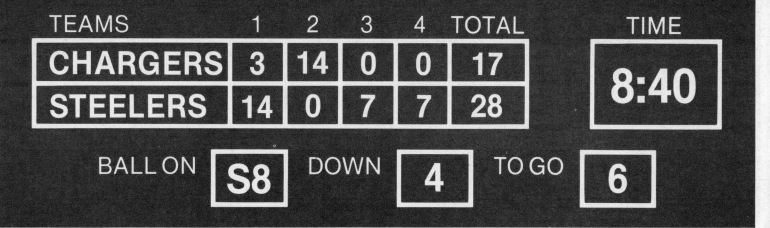

TEAMS	1	2	3	4	TOTAL
CHARGERS	3	14	0	0	17
STEELERS	14	0	7	7	28

TIME **8:40**

BALL ON **S8** DOWN **4** TO GO **6**

THE SITUATION   Dan Fouts, the Chargers' quarterback, is having one of his 300-yard days, but the Steelers have taken advantage of that weak San Diego defense. The Chargers have a chance to get back in the game, but they must get a touchdown, not a field goal.

You've got three big guns—Kellen Winslow, Wes Chandler, and Charlie Joiner—to throw to. It has got to be a good play because the Chargers may not get another opportunity like this. What do you do?

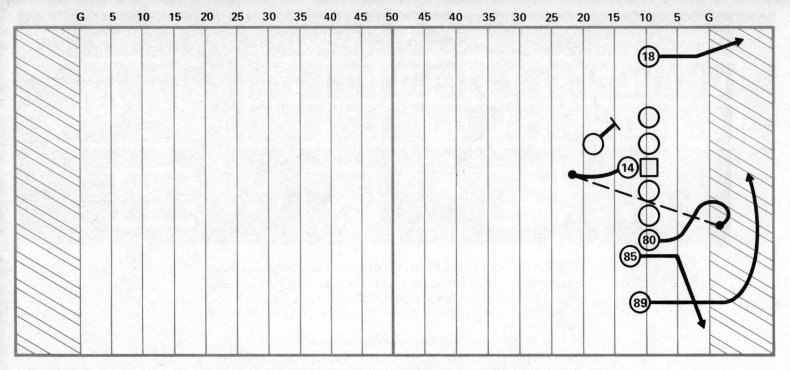

THE DECISION The pass, of course, is the call, and the lineup is full of receivers: Joiner (18) split left; Chandler (89) to the right; Winslow (80) at the tight end, and Eric Sievers (85), another tight end, playing in the slot behind and to the right of Winslow. The call by Fouts (14) is to Winslow, making use of his height and powerful movability in tight situations.

THE RESULT Winslow made a little move to the inside, went into the end zone, and hooked around to get the ball for a touchdown. (Another play from this game follows.)

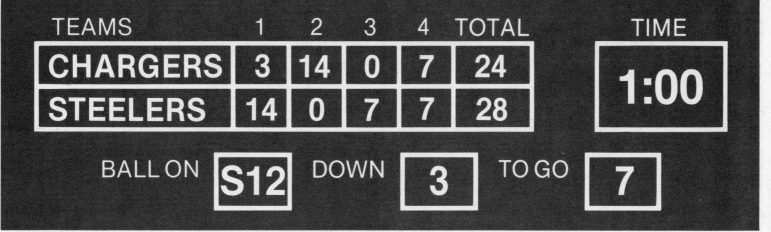

TEAMS	1	2	3	4	TOTAL
CHARGERS	3	14	0	7	24
STEELERS	14	0	7	7	28

TIME 1:00

BALL ON **S12**   DOWN **3**   TO GO **7**

THE SITUATION The Chargers are on the verge of a great comeback and have a chance to pull it out on this series of downs. But with third and 7, there is not much choice but to go for it all. Only a minute is left and the chance of seeing the ball again is nil if this drive fails.

The Chargers have their choice of a lot of weapons, not just the receivers but also runners like Chuck Muncie and James Brooks.

Do you go with the standard stuff here or something different?

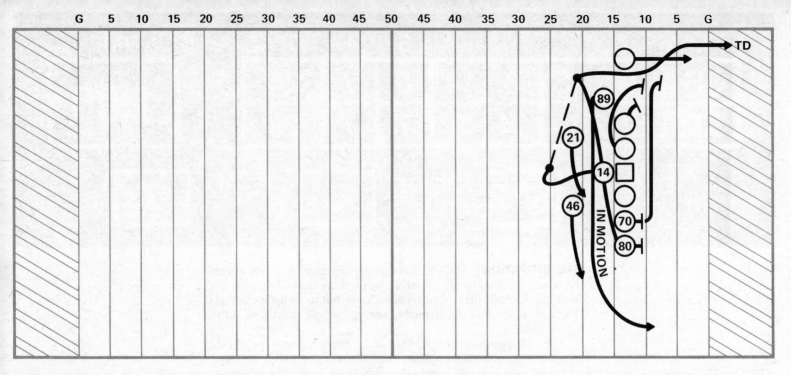

THE DECISION The call is for a screen pass to Kellen Winslow (80). It is complicated, but the Chargers have used it before, including once in this game. It is a gutsy play because there are many ways for it to fail, and a team has got to be thinking about the clock and the down at this juncture in the game.

The call is for Dan Fouts (14) to lead the opponent to believe Brooks (21) and Muncie (46) are teaming to sweep to the right. Winslow himself makes a block on the man in front of him before releasing to sneak through the line and over to the left flank. Russ

Washington (70), the right tackle, makes a block, too, before releasing to go pick up Winslow. The man-in-motion, Wes Chandler (89), has an important job leading the defense to distraction.

THE RESULT Winslow's great talents make this play. It is not easy getting through a crowd in the line and having your timing just perfect to pick up Washington's blocking. But Winslow does, and after catching the ball, he runs like a fullback down the left sideline for a touchdown.

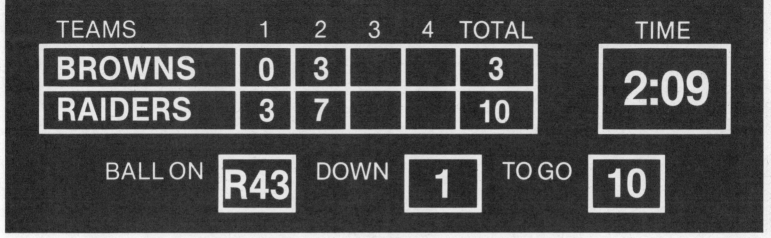

TEAMS	1	2	3	4	TOTAL	TIME
BROWNS	0	3			3	2:09
RAIDERS	3	7			10	

BALL ON **R43** DOWN **1** TO GO **10**

THE SITUATION The Browns seem overmatched in this playoff game against the Raiders, a team that had the best record in the AFC. But the Browns are still in the ball game and moving. They are around midfield with a first and 10 and have a lot of options. Paul McDonald has been the quarterback, ahead of Brian Sipe.

This is a pretty good chance to be a freewheeler with your play. What do you call?

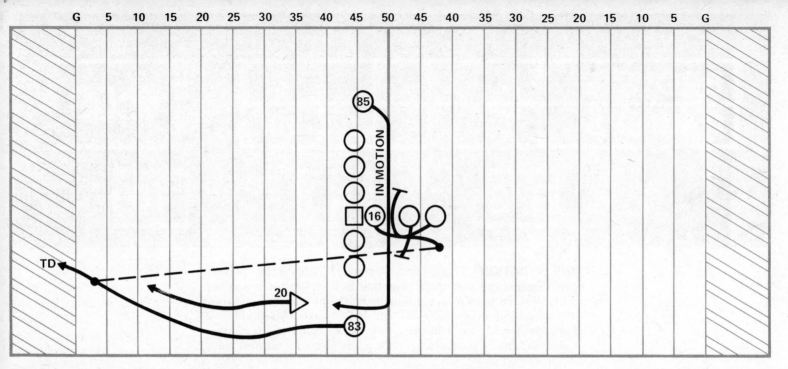

THE DECISION Ricky Feacher (83), the wide receiver left, is a flier. He averages about 19 yards a catch and has already had one good reception that set up the Browns' field goal in this game. The call is for a fake handoff to the deep back, a little confusion by Dave Logan (85) coming around in motion, but a straight fly pattern by Feacher. McDonald (16) makes the fake handoff to buy some time as Feacher gets downfield and then heaves him the ball.

THE RESULT A masterpiece. Feacher beat Ted Watts (20) and caught the ball on the 3-yard line to go in for the touchdown. After the extra point, the game was tied at 10–10. (Another play from this game follows.)

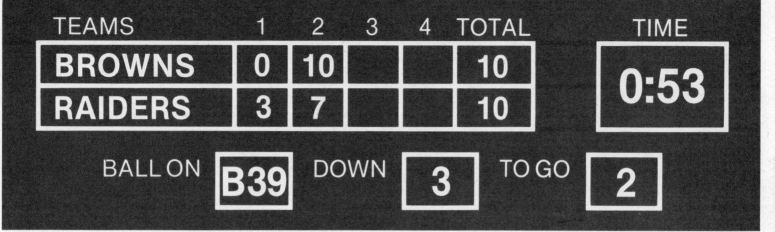

TEAMS	1	2	3	4	TOTAL	TIME
BROWNS	0	10			10	0:53
RAIDERS	3	7			10	

BALL ON **B39** DOWN **3** TO GO **2**

THE SITUATION Despite the Browns' previous score and time running out in the half, the Raiders get a drive going. But it is a precarious situation because they are out of timeouts and there are only seconds left in the half. They've got to make up their minds whether to go for broke and try to get a touchdown or to get the ball close enough to kick a tie-breaking field goal. Either looks dim with time running down. On third down and 2, it is a make-or-break play. What do you call?

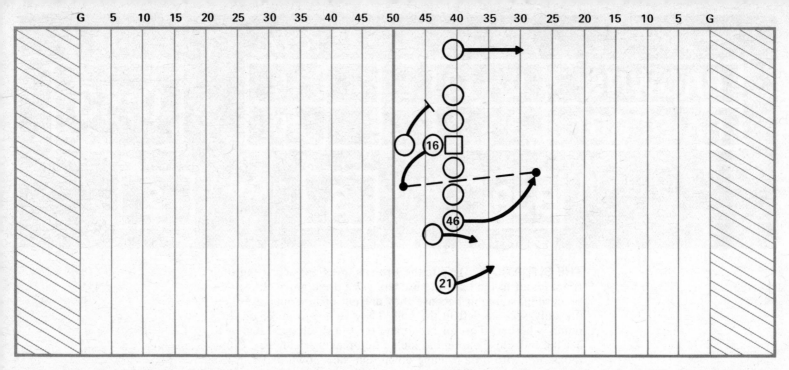

THE DECISION   The Raiders decide on what might be considered a surprise play. Todd Christensen (46) gets the call on a pass play over the middle. Even if Jim Plunkett (16) connects on the pass, the play is sure to eat up time, and don't forget that the Raiders are without a timeout. On this play, Plunkett looks long to Cliff Branch (21) downfield, then goes to Christensen over the middle.

THE RESULT   Perhaps because no one was expecting the Raiders to use up time on such a play, it was simple to be successful. Christensen caught the ball for a 12-yard gain on the Cleveland 27. And all worked out well for the Raiders: they made a field goal in the waning seconds of the half to take the lead.

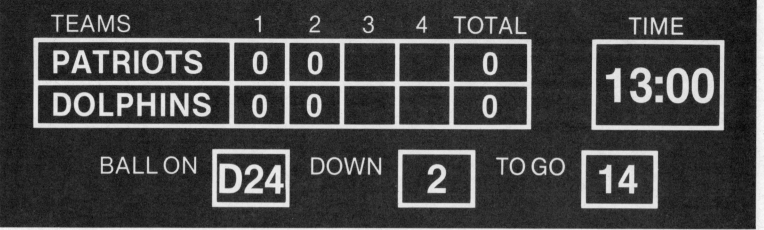

TEAMS	1	2	3	4	TOTAL	TIME
PATRIOTS	0	0			0	13:00
DOLPHINS	0	0			0	

BALL ON **D24**   DOWN **2**   TO GO **14**

THE SITUATION   The Patriots had mounted a good drive in the scoreless game even though Steve Grogan had not been passing well. It is second and long yardage and a fairly obvious passing situation. Preston Brown, Lin Dawson, and Stanley Morgan are your receivers. How do you utilize them against a Miami Dolphin defense that has been downright stingy all day?

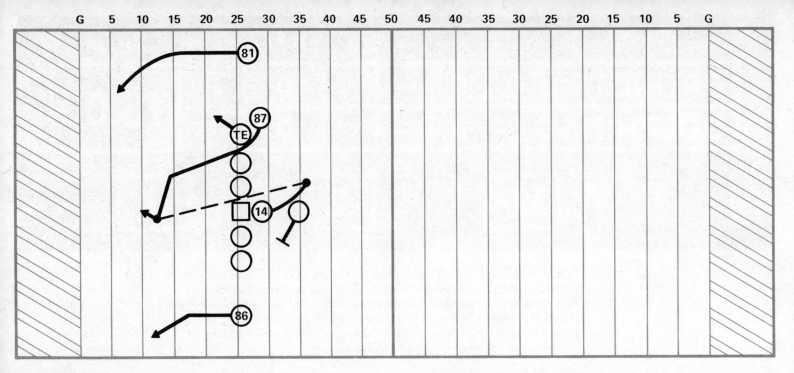

THE DECISION The play calls for Brown (81) and Morgan (86) to split wide but to draw attention away from the middle of the field. Dawson (87) is to cut inside of the tight end on the right side and get the pass from Grogan (14).

THE RESULT Dawson caught the ball for a first down on the Dolphins' 8-yard line. Good call, well executed by Dawson, who ran through a crowd to get to the ball. (Another play from this game follows.)

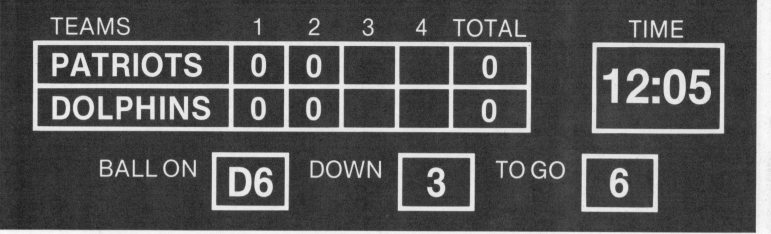

TEAMS	1	2	3	4	TOTAL
PATRIOTS	0	0			0
DOLPHINS	0	0			0

TIME **12:05**

BALL ON **D6**   DOWN **3**   TO GO **6**

THE SITUATION   With a first down from the previous play, the Patriots may be thinking upset. The Dolphins are very tough defensively, however. You don't get too many first downs inside the 10-yard line against them, so you better make some wise decisions. The Patriots' running attack, with Tony Collins and Mark van Eeghen, is okay but not overwhelming. The passing game is decent but not overwhelming. The best receiver, by far, is Stanley Morgan.

An additional problem on this particular play was the noise at the Orange Bowl, the Dolphins' home field.

Anyway, you have four downs to work the ball deep in Miami territory. What do you do with the first of those downs?

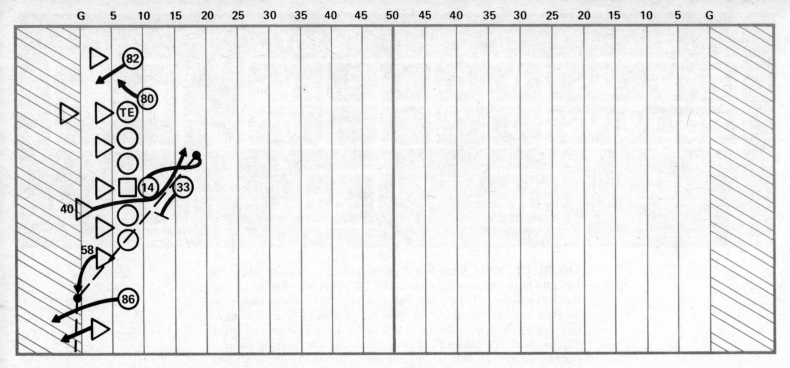

THE DECISION   Steve Grogan (14) had no easy choice because of the crowd noise. With the Miami defense set, he tried an audible, but it could not be heard. He did the next best thing: send someone downfield, in this case Stanley Morgan (86), and try to get the ball to him. If the odds are not good on that, throw it out of bounds.

THE RESULT   An out-of-bounds pass by Grogan, who threw it below Morgan, who was covered in the end zone. Smart play under the circumstances. (Another play from this game follows.)

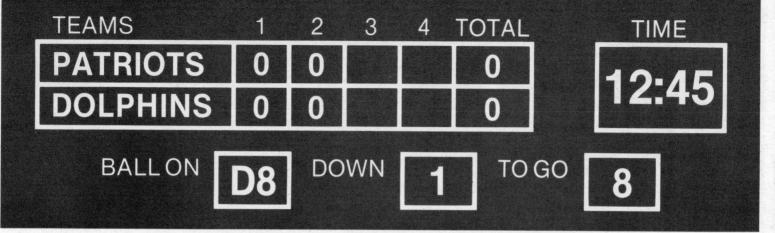

TEAMS	1	2	3	4	TOTAL
PATRIOTS	0	0			0
DOLPHINS	0	0			0

TIME **12:45**

BALL ON **D8**   DOWN **1**   TO GO **8**

THE SITUATION Two plays after Steve Grogan threw the ball out of bounds, the Patriots are still trying to punch the ball over the Miami goal line. The Dolphins just don't relent down this deep, and the Patriots have got to come up with something. The New England running game just isn't that strong on a third and goal, and the passing game has been weak most of the day.

But if you are going to beat Miami and move along in the playoffs, you have to score under these circumstances, so what kind of a play can you come up with?

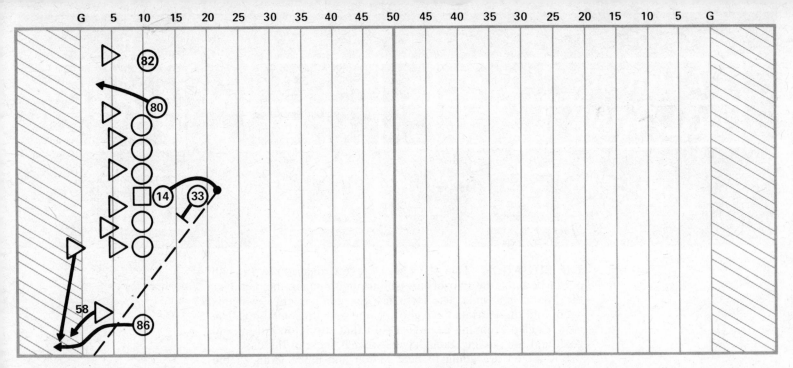

THE DECISION The Patriots load up the lineup with receivers—Morgan (86) wide to the left, Ken Toler (82) to the wide right, and Don Hasselbeck (80) in the slot behind the tight end. Tony Collins (33) is the lone running back. But the call is to go to Morgan shooting down the left sideline, similar to the play in which Steve Grogan (14) threw the ball out of bounds on first down.

THE RESULT The Dolphins read this routine play rather easily. Kim Bokamper (58) was back to knock down the pass after Mike Kozlowski (40) of the Dolphins put a tremendous safety-blitz scare into Grogan and made him hurry his throw. The Patriots had to settle for a field goal on the next play and never did mount much of an offense all day long as Miami won the game, 28–13.

COMMERCIAL TIME-OUT! 300

SCOTT BRUNNER

JIM PLUNKETT

JOE MONTANA

DAN FOUTS

KEN ANDERSON

TOMMY KRAMER

RON JAWORSKI

For decades, one of football's statistical staples has been the runner who gains more than 100 yards in a game. In the NFL, on any given week, that is not an unusual achievement, though a very good one. Over a player's career, however, it is not that frequent. Jim Brown did it a record 58 times. But except for an occasional Jim Brown, O. J. Simpson, or Walter Payton, hardly any player can sustain a 100-yard average over the course of a season. George Rogers managed the feat in 1981, but just barely.

Perhaps an even more important yardstick for game-breakers has emerged in recent years. And that is the plethora of 300-yards-a-game passers.

It doesn't take a statistical genius to figure out that any team would rather have 300-yard games than 100, but until the volume of 300-yard passers emerged in recent seasons, that figure went little noticed compared with 100-yard rushers.

Then came Dan Fouts of the San Diego Chargers. In 1980, Fouts passed for 300 yards or more in eight different games, an NFL record. In 1981, he had seven such games, second best to his own record. In 1982, a nine-game season, he had five 300-yard games to tie Joe Montana of the San Francisco 49ers for the league lead.

But Fouts and Montana were not the only long-gainers of the 1982 season. The league records showed that 20 different quarterbacks achieved the 300-yard plateau a total of 36 times. By way of comparison, 25 different runners gained 100 or more yards rushing 47 times. While three quarterbacks passed for 300 yards on at least four different occasions, no runner gained 100 yards more than three times.

Fouts has become such a dominating figure as a passer that he has averaged 290 yards passing over the past 60 games. And in the 1982 season, he surpassed Johnny Unitas as the top man in most 300-yard games during a career. Fouts has 30, Unitas had 26.

300-YARD-PASSING GAMES, 1982 SEASON

5   Dan Fouts, San Diego

5   Joe Montana, San Francisco

4   Ken Anderson, Cincinnati

3   Jim Plunkett, L.A. Raiders

2   Scott Brunner, N.Y. Giants

2   Ron Jaworski, Philadelphia

2   Tommy Kramer, Minnesota

1 each: Paul McDonald, Cleveland; Doug Williams, Tampa Bay; Vince Ferragamo, L.A. Rams; Gary Danielson, Detroit; Steve DeBerg, Denver; Ken Stabler, New Orleans; Brian Sipe, Cleveland; Richard Todd, N.Y. Jets; Jim Zorn, Seattle; Joe Ferguson, Buffalo; Danny White, Dallas; Joe Theismann, Washington, and Steve Bartkowski, Atlanta.

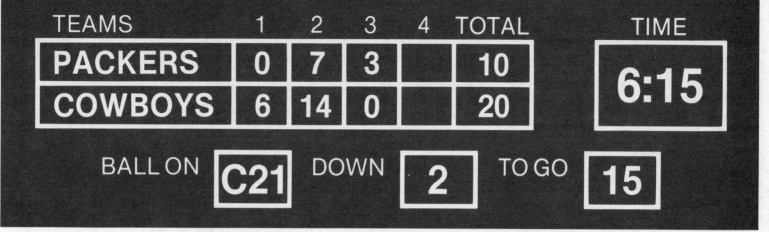

TEAMS	1	2	3	4	TOTAL	TIME
PACKERS	0	7	3		10	6:15
COWBOYS	6	14	0		20	

BALL ON **C21** DOWN **2** TO GO **15**

THE SITUATION The Packers have a chance to narrow the Dallas Cowboys' margin, but it is a tough call with second down and 15. Lynn Dickey, the Green Bay quarterback, is having a good passing day, and James Lofton is on his way to gaining more than 100 yards as a receiver. John Jefferson is the other outstanding Packer long threat, and Paul Coffman, the tight end, is capable of making the 15-yarder the Packers need. The best running back is Eddie Lee Ivery. What play do you call?

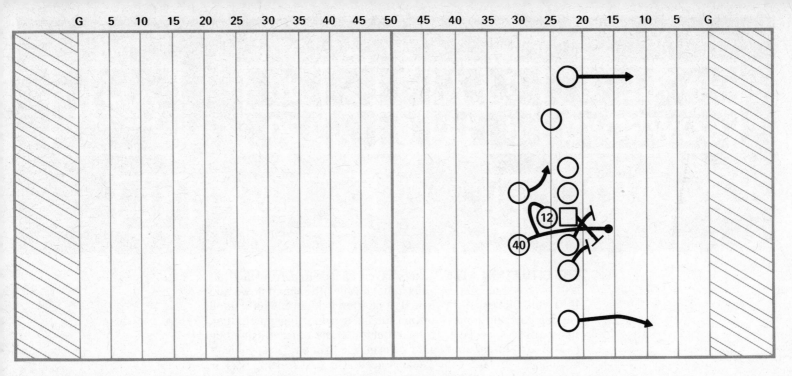

G	5	10	15	20	25	30	35	40	45	50	45	40	35	30	25	20	15	10	5	G

THE DECISION   Somewhat strangely, the Packers went to Eddie Lee Ivery (40) on a simple handoff from Lynn Dickey (12). Nothing special, just power blocking to get him through the hole between right guard and center.

THE RESULT   A mere 5-yard gain at an important point in the game, for a team that needed a couple of big scores. (Another play from this game follows.)

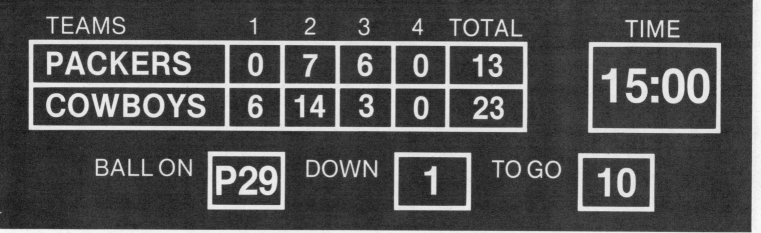

TEAMS	1	2	3	4	TOTAL	TIME
PACKERS	0	7	6	0	13	15:00
COWBOYS	6	14	3	0	23	

BALL ON **P29** DOWN **1** TO GO **10**

THE SITUATION The Packers are moving the ball well but not getting the big plays to break something open. Telltale time is coming up, as this is the first play of the final quarter and Green Bay is deep in its own territory. It seems that the Pack has to spring James Lofton or John Jefferson, its two great receivers, on something long. How do they do it?

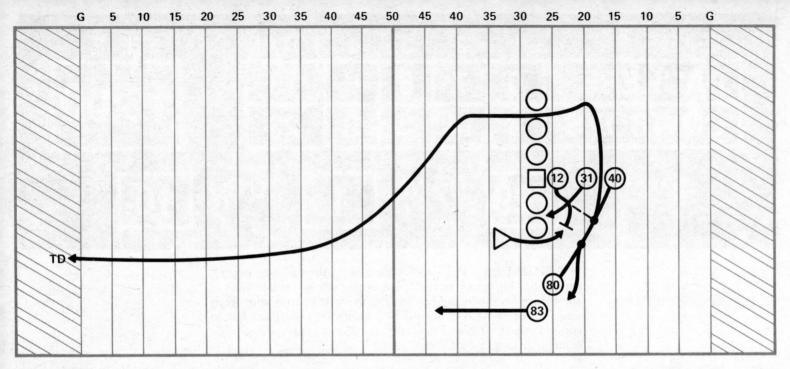

THE DECISION   This is a James Lofton special. The Packers line up in the I-formation, with Lynn Dickey (12) over center and Eddie Lee Ivery (40) and Gerry Ellis (31) the backs. John Jefferson (83) is on the left side wide, with Lofton (80) between him and the left tackle. The play is supposed to have Ellis leading Ivery into the line on the left side, with Dickey taking a step or two back before pitching out to Ivery. Ivery takes the pitch but hands to Lofton coming around. The defense by now is heavily weighted to its right side, opening up the Packers' right side to Lofton coming around.

THE RESULT   A speedy, twisting 71-yard touchdown for Lofton, who just scampered away from the Dallas defense. It was the second time of the season that he pulled off this play for a touchdown. (Another play from this game follows.)

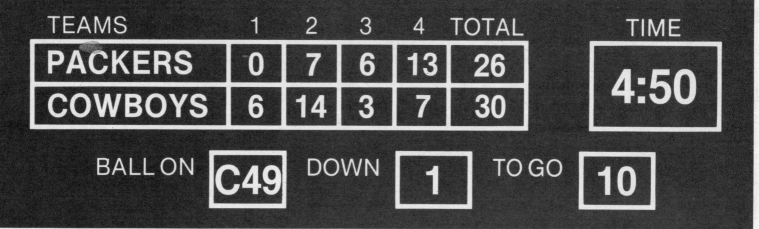

TEAMS	1	2	3	4	TOTAL	TIME
PACKERS	0	7	6	13	26	4:50
COWBOYS	6	14	3	7	30	

BALL ON **C49**   DOWN **1**   TO GO **10**

THE SITUATION   The Cowboys have the ball at midfield, and it seems that they have to play the clock. If they do it well, they are on their way to the conference championship again. But from midfield, that is not as easy as it looks. With almost 5 minutes remaining, it is obvious they may have to put the ball in the air a few more times as well as use their runners, like Tony Dorsett, to eat up the clock. This is an interesting situation because of the first and 10 and the need to keep the ball moving. Any of a number of plays could be chosen. Which one would you call?

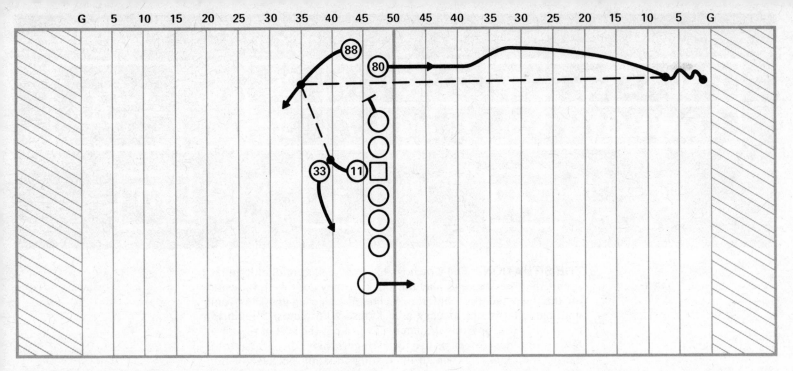

THE DECISION With Danny White (11) the quarterback and Tony Dorsett (33) the lone running back, the Cowboys spread the receivers wide. Drew Pearson (88) and Tony Hill (80) are flooding the right side. But the play selection is a wild one, calling for White to lateral overhand to Pearson, who has dropped back about 7 yards behind the line of scrimmage. Then Pearson wings a long pass downfield to Hill.

THE RESULT Pearson, a former high school quarterback, did it perfectly, and Hill managed to get down to the 7-yard line where he caught the ball and carried it to the 1. The Cowboys scored on the next play and won this game, 37–26.

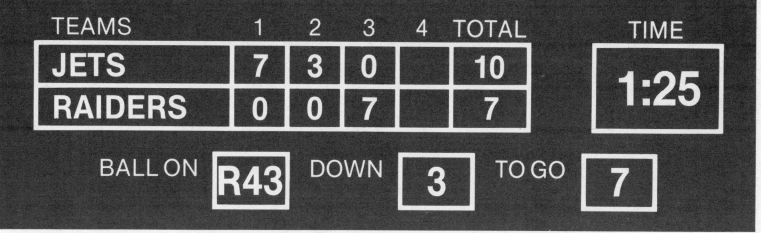

TEAMS	1	2	3	4	TOTAL	TIME
JETS	7	3	0		10	
RAIDERS	0	0	7		7	1:25

BALL ON R43 **DOWN** 3 **TO GO** 7

THE SITUATION In a bitter game between the Jets and the Raiders, two teams that have had some nasty battles over the years, finesse is still sharing the spotlight with aggressiveness. The low scoring does not reflect the fact that both teams were moving the ball fairly well in this game. The Raiders line up on this play after a couple of conservative ploys, a screen pass to their brilliant rookie, Marcus Allen, and then a run by Allen. The two plays have put the Raiders in a hole, and they need passing yardage to control the ball. Quarterback Jim Plunkett's big weapons are Cliff Branch and Malcolm Barnwell. Branch usually gets a steady diet of Plunkett passes; Barnwell, the potential long-gainers. Todd Christensen, a converted running back, is the tight end, and he can catch, too. What should the Raiders do in this low-scoring contest?

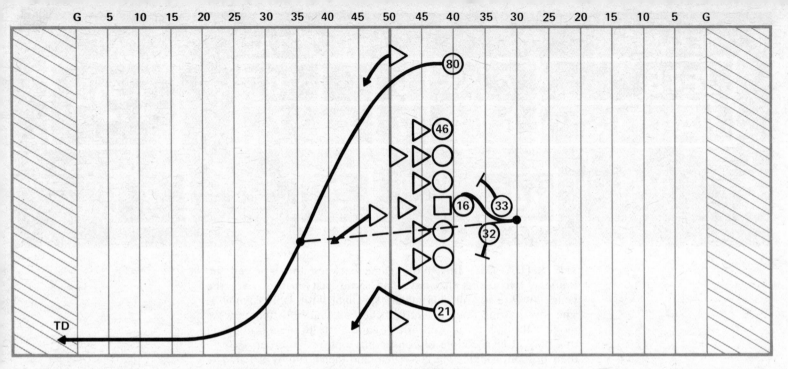

THE DECISION Go long, Jim Plunkett (16) to Malcolm Barnwell (80). Kenny King (33) is in the backfield to block for Plunkett and Marcus Allen (32) is a potential safety valve if Barnwell is covered, as is Todd Christensen (46). Cliff Branch (21) just does a short pattern to keep the defense from spreading backward after Barnwell gets downfield.

THE RESULT Barnwell made a great move getting across the Jet defense. He caught the ball on the Jets' 35, ran to the sideline at about the 30, and was home free—a 57-yard touchdown. (Another play from this game follows.)

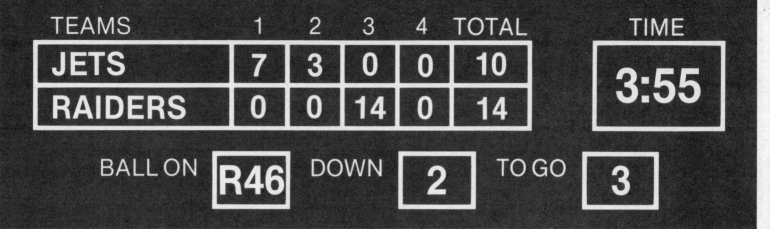

TEAMS	1	2	3	4	TOTAL	TIME
JETS	7	3	0	0	10	3:55
RAIDERS	0	0	14	0	14	

BALL ON **R46** DOWN **2** TO GO **3**

THE SITUATION With the Los Angeles Raiders in the lead and time winding down, the New York Jets need a big play, just as the Raiders did in the previous period. Richard Todd's passing game has been solid, magnified by some great catches by Wesley Walker. The running game is solid, too, paced by Freeman McNeil, the league's leading rusher. Lam Jones has caught a couple of long-gainers, and McNeil is capable of picking up passing yardage, too. With a second-and-3 situation, the Jets can try a variety of plays. They have the edge over the defense here. What should they call?

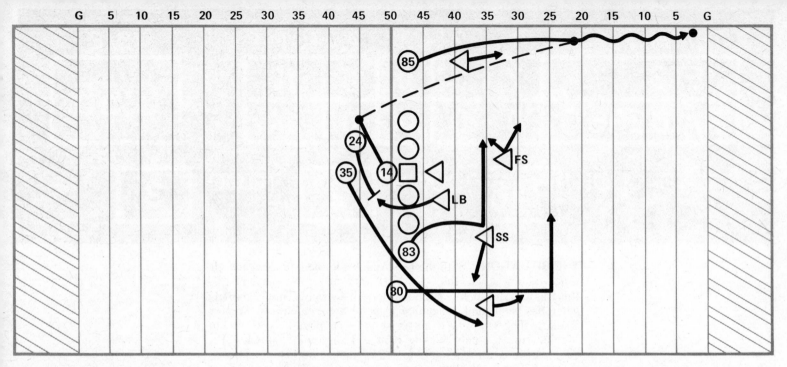

THE DECISION With Lam Jones (80) as the flanker to the right and Wesley Walker (85) the wide receiver left, the Jets are ready to travel. With Jerome Barkum (83), the tight end, and the two running backs, Freeman McNeil (24) and Mike Augustyniak (35), in the game, Richard Todd (14) must have the Raiders befuddled on a second and 3. The target is Walker, however, after all the commotion on the right side of the center.

THE RESULT Walker just made his mad dash down the field and caught the ball on the fly. He made 45 yards to the Raiders' 1-yard line, and the Jets later scored the go-ahead touchdown. (Another play from this game follows.)

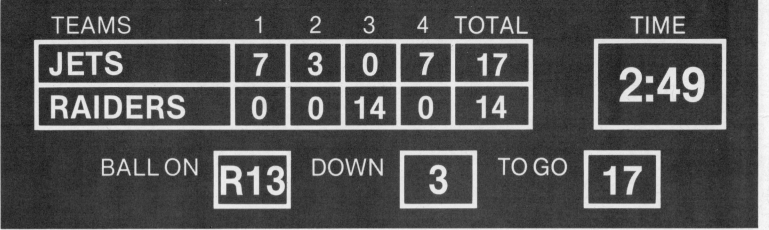

TEAMS	1	2	3	4	TOTAL	TIME
JETS	7	3	0	7	17	2:49
RAIDERS	0	0	14	0	14	

BALL ON **R13** DOWN **3** TO GO **17**

THE SITUATION The Raiders are regrouping after losing their lead to the Jets. It's a long way to the Jets' goal line, but all the Raiders need is a field goal to put the game into overtime. There is enough time. But Jim Plunkett must first get the Raiders out of this hole. What should the Raiders call?

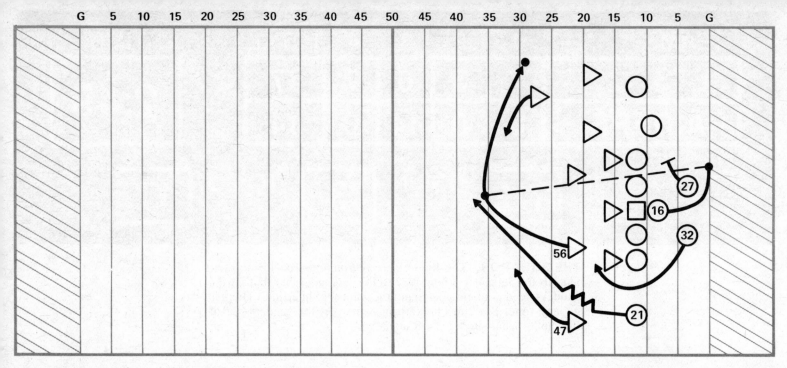

THE DECISION Jim Plunkett (16) lines up with Marcus Allen (32) and Frank Hawkins (27) behind him. Cliff Branch (21) is split to the left. The call is for a pass over the middle to Branch breaking across. It's a Plunkett specialty, and Branch makes it a potential breakaway play because of his moves and his speed.

THE RESULT The Jets' Jerry Holmes (47) tried to follow Branch across the middle, but Lance Mehl (56), a linebacker dropping deep, saw the ball coming. Mehl made the interception on the 35-yard line and returned it 7 more yards. (Another play from this game follows.)

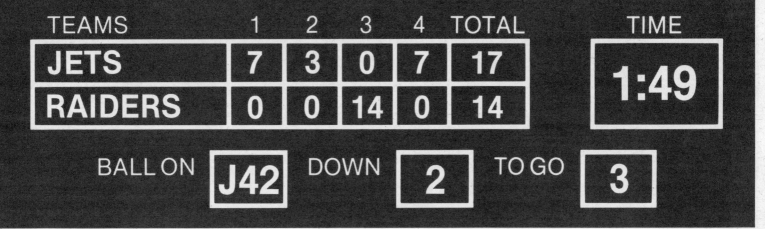

TEAMS	1	2	3	4	TOTAL	TIME
JETS	7	3	0	7	17	1:49
RAIDERS	0	0	14	0	14	

BALL ON **J42** DOWN **2** TO GO **3**

THE SITUATION The Jets had this game in their grasp after Lance Mehl's interception, only to have Freeman McNeil fumble away the ball as they were killing the clock. That gave the ball back to the Raiders with less than 2 minutes left. Jim Plunkett got the Raiders going upfield, to the Jets' 42. The tying field goal, if not a winning touchdown, was looming as a possibility for Los Angeles. With second down and 3, all Plunkett has to do is keep the drive going. What should his team call?

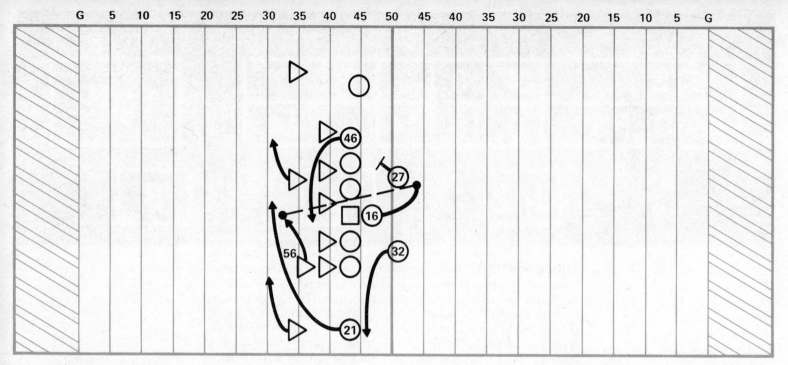

THE DECISION The Raiders liked the way Cliff Branch (21) pulled away from the Jets' Jerry Holmes on the interception. They call the same type of play, with Marcus Allen (32) and Frank Hawkins (27) in the backfield with Jim Plunkett (16). Todd Christensen (46), the tight end, goes low on this pattern, while Branch goes high.

THE RESULT Needing only 3 yards on this play, Plunkett got a little greedy and went to Branch breaking over center. Christensen was clearly in the open coming from the other side and surely would have made the first down. Again, Lance Mehl (56) of the Jets dropped back and picked off the pass. This time the Jets killed the clock and won the game, 17–14.

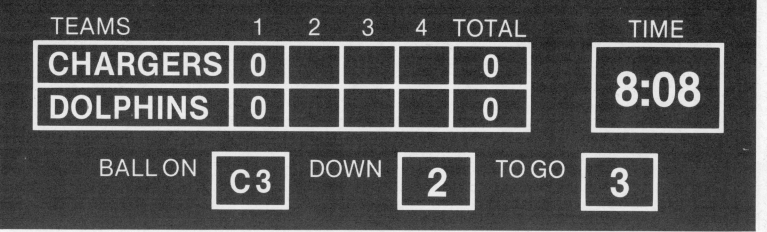

TEAMS	1	2	3	4	TOTAL	TIME
CHARGERS	0				0	8:08
DOLPHINS	0				0	

BALL ON C 3   **DOWN** 2   **TO GO** 3

THE SITUATION Against the high-scoring San Diego Chargers, even a fine defensive team like the Miami Dolphins wants to get on the scoreboard first. What Miami had going for it in this game was the weak San Diego defense. The Dolphins were striking quickly on this drive, and it seemed just a question of what play to call to get the ball into the end zone. David Woodley, the Dolphin quarterback, is dangerous in such situations because he throws well from the rollout and is a threat to run the ball in himself. He has a pair of good short-yardage runners in Andra Franklin and Tony Nathan. And his tight ends, Ronnie Lee and Bruce Hardy, are tough near the goal line, too. With a couple of downs to play with, what do you call?

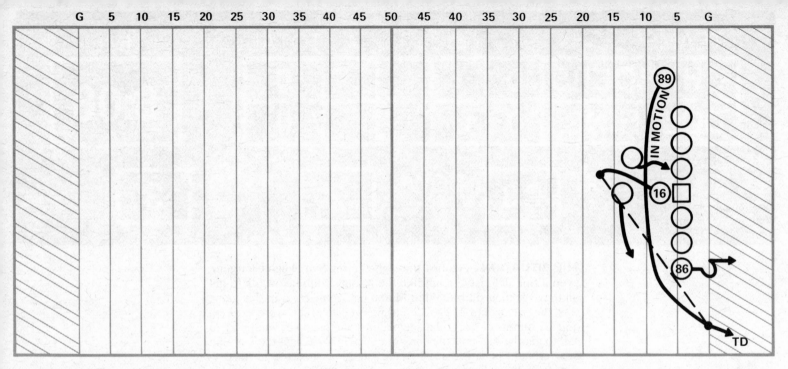

THE DECISION Nat Moore (89), the wide receiver to the left, comes all the way around on the man-in-motion as David Woodley (16) takes his time with the count. Woodley won't roll out that much on this play, hoping to stay back and pick out Moore or his tight end Ronnie Lee (86), who goes to the goal line and acts as a safety valve.

THE RESULT Moore, after his long pattern, caught the ball right on the goal line and stepped in for the touchdown. Lee made a nice play here, too, virtually backing toward the goal line after a couple of steps forward. The Dolphins just kept on scoring in this game, rolling up a 24–0 lead, and won 34–13.

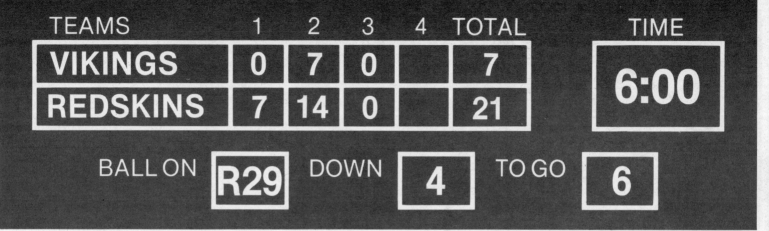

TEAMS	1	2	3	4	TOTAL	TIME
VIKINGS	0	7	0		7	6:00
REDSKINS	7	14	0		21	

BALL ON **R29**   DOWN **4**   TO GO **6**

THE SITUATION   The Washington Redskins hold a comfortable lead against the Minnesota Vikings, who have the ball. The Vikings had a heartbreaker when Sammy White, their fine receiver, dropped a ball in the end zone on third down and 1. A penalty has put the Vikings back another 5 yards, so it is long yardage on fourth down. But the Vikings decide to go for it. What should they call?

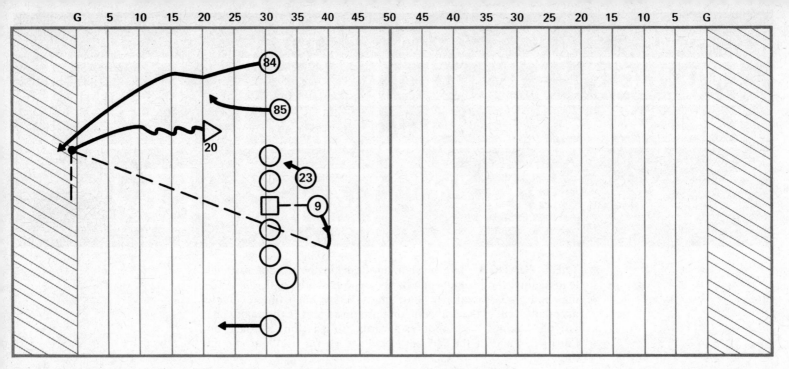

THE DECISION The Vikings load up the strong side with Sam McCullum (84) and Sammy White (85), and the quarterback, Tommy Kramer (9) goes into the shotgun, with Ted Brown (23) alongside him. It is just a mow-'em-down play, with McCullum making a couple of fakes and heading for the post.

THE RESULT Joe Lavender (20), a Redskin cornerback, dropped back with McCullum and managed to knock down the ball. (Another play from this game follows.)

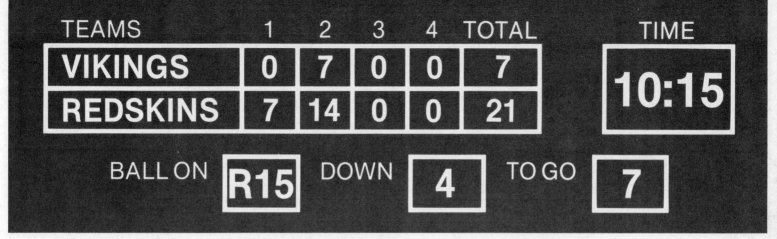

TEAMS	1	2	3	4	TOTAL	TIME
VIKINGS	0	7	0	0	7	10:15
REDSKINS	7	14	0	0	21	

BALL ON **R15**   DOWN **4**   TO GO **7**

THE SITUATION Still early in the fourth quarter, the Vikings have gotten themselves into another fourth down and long, but it is down on the Redskins' 15, and they want to go for it. A field goal won't make much of a dent in Washington's 14-point lead. What should they do to get the 7 yards?

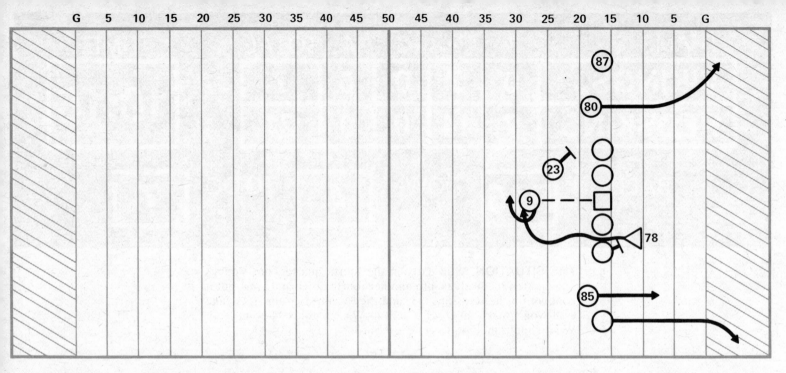

THE DECISION   Tommy Kramer (9) again goes into the shotgun, with Ted Brown (23) off to his left in the backfield. He's got Terry LeCount (80), Sammy White (85), and Leo Lewis (87) in the game to catch the ball, so he has his choice of receivers.

THE RESULT   In such a tight corner, the Redskins managed to pick up most of Kramer's receivers, and he got sacked by Tony McGee (78) while he was looking for a free target. (Another play from this game follows.)

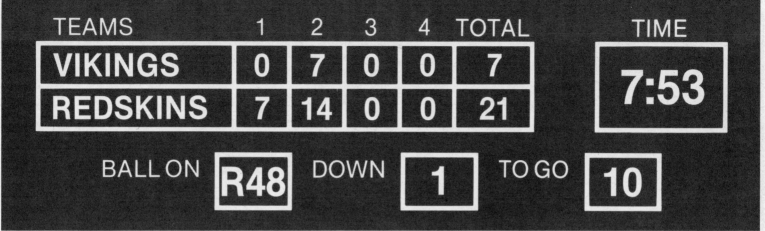

TEAMS	1	2	3	4	TOTAL
VIKINGS	0	7	0	0	7
REDSKINS	7	14	0	0	21

TIME

7:53

BALL ON R48   DOWN 1   TO GO 10

THE SITUATION The Redskins have been in front of the Vikings all the way in this game, but another score for insurance would be nice. After all, there are almost 8 minutes to eat up, and the Vikings have made a few threats. It is always safe to give the ball to John Riggins on a first and 10, especially in this game where he has carried almost three dozen times at about 5 yards a try. Joe Theismann hasn't had to pass too much, and he has kept to the shorter stuff with a higher completion percentage. Now it is time to decide whether to really play it safe at midfield or try to penetrate for another score. What do you do?

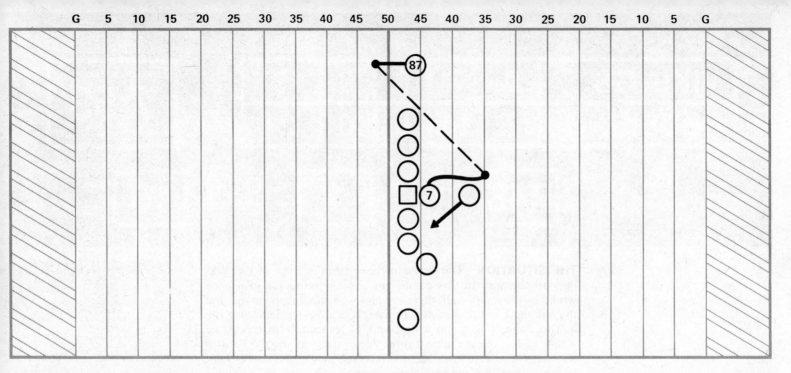

THE DECISION A fairly routine decision—a pass from Joe Theismann (7) to Charlie Brown (87). Brown's route was not too far from the line of scrimmage, protecting against an interception. He just went down the right side.

THE RESULT A safe play, which tried possibly to spring Brown loose and at the same time pick up some yardage while giving Riggins a break. It went for 4 yards, and the Redskins went back to feeding Riggins the ball to kill the clock.

HALFTIME
HALFTIME
HALFTIME

the tournament bracket diagram

SUPER BOWL XVII TOURNAMENT

FIRST ROUND

SEMI-FINALS

NFC

Redskins 31
Lions 7

Vikings 30
Falcons 24

Redskins 21
Vikings 7

NFC CHAMPIONSHIP

Packers 41
Cardinals 16

Cowboys 30
Buccaneers 17

Cowboys 37
Packers 26

Redskins 31
Cowboys 17

SUPER BOWL XVII

Redskins 27
Dolphins 17

AFC

Dolphins 28
Patriots 13

Chargers 31
Steelers 28

Dolphins 34
Chargers 13

Dolphins 14
Jets 0

Jets 44
Bengals 17

Raiders 27
Browns 10

Jets 17
Raiders 14

AFC CHAMPIONSHIP

DEE-FENSE

In World War II, college football began playing two-platoon football through necessity. There were not enough good football players to go both ways, as football had almost always been played. The 60-minute player went out before the end of the 1940s, and the two sets of 30-minute players came in (one platoon for offense, one for defense). From these college players came the specialists, who modernized professional football in the 1950s.

But with special coaches and special techniques for defense, the defenses of some teams began to dominate just as offensive teams used to do.

And with more time to spend on defense, the techniques became so intricate that before too long the defenses were dictating what the offensive opponents should do. Furthermore, the professional game has evolved today whereby offensive strategies are changing almost annually to keep ahead of the ever-changing defenses.

If there is one word to describe the change in defenses in the past 30 years, it would be "sophistication."

FIRST DEFENSE

The original formations on defense were basic, to counteract the offenses. Against a T-formation, for example, the defense would line up in a 7-1-2-1 alignment, sometimes overstacking its power to a team that constantly ran its power plays to one area.

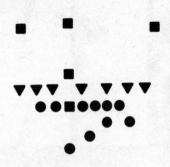

THE OKLAHOMA

The University of Oklahoma, with many more talented linemen in the days of two-platoon football, found it could get by with only five linemen, giving the team extra linebackers and defensive backs who could roam to adjust for players in motion on offense.

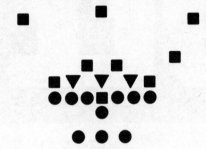

THE 5-3

The 5-3 defense had five down linemen and three deep backs. It was really a 5-3-3, and it was used to counteract more passing plays.

EAGLE DEFENSE

The Philadelphia Eagle defense gave an umbrella effect, but it became vulnerable to any team passing over the middle.

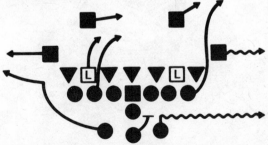

THE UMBRELLA

A refinement of the Eagle defense was the Umbrella, designed by Steve Owens, coach of the New York Giants and helped along by his assistant, Tom Landry. With a linebacker back in the middle, it was not as vulnerable to the short pass behind the line of scrimmage and in front of the deep backs.

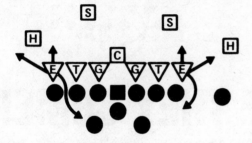

EAGLE UPDATE
A short-lived update of the original Eagle defense, before the Umbrella came into vogue.

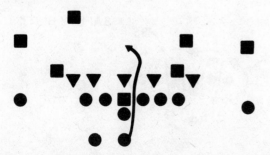

Football teams with better defensive linemen found they could use their linebackers more effectively by placing them back.

THE 4-3

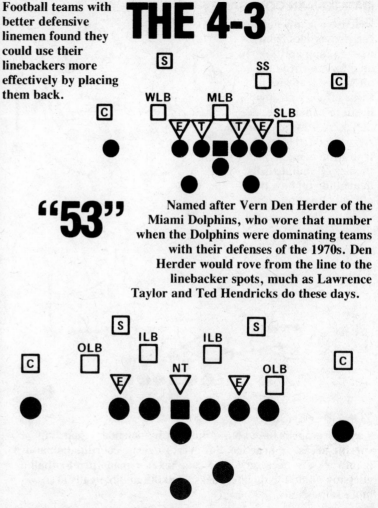

"53"

Named after Vern Den Herder of the Miami Dolphins, who wore that number when the Dolphins were dominating teams with their defenses of the 1970s. Den Herder would rove from the line to the linebacker spots, much as Lawrence Taylor and Ted Hendricks do these days.

141

MAN-TO-MAN COVERAGE

Defensive teams mix up their coverages from man-to-man and zone in an effort to check the offensive strategies if those offensive teams begin to believe the defensive units are too stereotyped. The transition is made with the use of audible calls, depending on how the offenses line up.

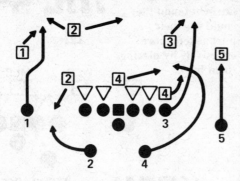

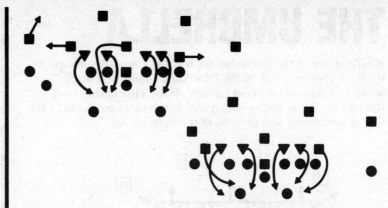

HERE THEY COME!

The defenses of the 1980s are bound to change, just as defenses have been revolutionized almost yearly since the 1940s. Look for a variety of blitzes, of men on defense swarming the offenses from every-which direction.

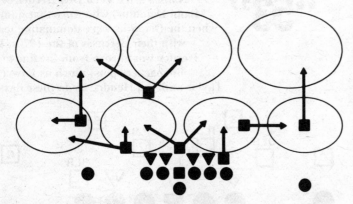

ZONE DEFENSE

Zone coverage is based on, quite simply, defenders guarding specific areas. In practice, however, intricate coordination and teamwork are necessary. The zone defense made pro football a guessing game for quarterbacks, making audible calls even more important.

SAFETY BLITZ

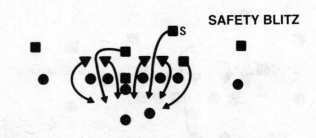

trickery, fakery, or kickery?

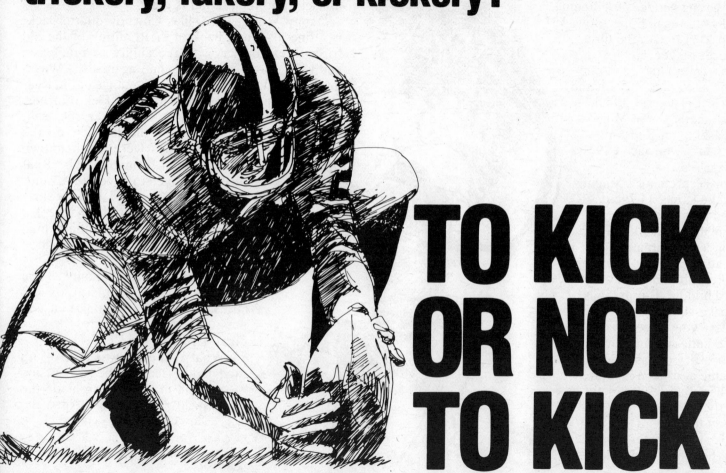

TO KICK OR NOT TO KICK

In the highly sophisticated planning of professional football, the thought of having the ball in the wrong hands is frightening. One only has to recall Super Bowl VII, when Garo Yepremian, the little former soccer player, had his field-goal attempt blocked at midfield and he picked up the ball and tried to pass it. The errant ball ended up in the hands of Mike Bass, a Washington Redskins defensive back, who raced 49 yards for a giveaway touchdown. Yepremian's Miami team won the game, 14-7, but some blood pressures rose.

Even a planned fake kick, whether on a punt situation or a field-goal attempt, stands out in pro football like something out of a schoolyard huddle. But in the NFL's strange strike-shortened 1982 season, teams were trying to get an edge in any way they could, and there was an abundance of trickery on fake kicks. Most, of course, came at crucial junctures in games, where failures stand out more prominently.

For many teams, the fake punt for a run is at the punter's discretion. When the defenders turn en masse to go downfield to block for their kick-returner, the punter often has a wide-open field to himself, and temptation is great.

Danny White, the Dallas Cowboy quarterback, is a fine all-round back in the tradition of the old triple-threat backs, with the ability to run, pass, and kick. So in one 1982 game, against the Washington Redskins, White took advantage of the Redskins' decision to peel back for their kick returner.

The situation was this: Dallas was in the lead, 17-10, with little more than 8 minutes left on the clock. The Cowboys were on their own 7-yard line, in punt formation. The Redskins must have loved to have White punting from that deep a hole late in a close game. But when three Redskins peeled back too quickly after their contain man overran White, the Dallas punter just took off and followed them.

What was he thinking about? "You don't think about it until it's over," White said. "Then you think that you must be crazy. Obviously, I have a crazy streak in me."

What White did was take off up the middle, leaving the two outside rushers in a bind. He made the first down, and that helped the Cowboys run down the clock for more than 2 minutes and give White a chance

TO KICK...

to punt later from a more advantageous field position. The Cowboys went on to inflict the only defeat on Washington all season long, though Cowboy Coach Tom Landry, the conservative Texan, did admit later, "I almost fainted," when White took off on his run.

Teams do practice the fake punt almost every week, but it has been a rare moment when it is used. Yet in a more planned fake than White's, Russell Erxleben of the New Orleans Saints tossed a 39-yard touchdown pass from punt formation in the last week of the season when the Saints were trying desperately for a playoff berth.

And the most daring fake punt of all was tried by the Miami Dolphins when they were protecting a 27-13 lead against the high-scoring San Diego Chargers in the 1982 playoffs.

Tom Orosz, the Dolphin punter, had been known to take off on a sprint before. He had faked one and ran for 13 yards to keep a field-goal drive going late in the 1981 season. His first down helped lead to the field goal, breaking a 7-7 tie with the Kansas City Chiefs in a game that the Dolphins won, 17-7.

In the 1982 game, the Chargers apparently had stymied the Miami offense on the Dolphins' 29-yard line, forcing a fourth-down-and-1 situation. As he took the snap and prepared to kick, Orosz noticed that all of the Chargers were dropping back to set up a wall of blockers for their return man, James Brooks. He just took the ball under his arm and started to head for the left. Orosz picked up 11 yards before he was tackled.

Though his heady play did not lead to a touchdown, the Dolphins mounted a good drive and got out of trouble.

Steve Crosby, the Dolphins' special-teams coach, estimated later that on a fake punt, the chances for success may not be as difficult as they appear. He said the opponents are vulnerable about 75 percent of the time because they are so busy thinking return. But Crosby or any other coach knows that failure on a fake can be an outright disaster for the kicking team.

Yepremian excepted, the fake field goal is by design. Occasionally, there will be a bad snap or a fumble by the holder that will force a team into a last-second pass or run. (Mike Wood of the Baltimore Colts had a 5-yard touchdown pass after a broken field goal against the Dolphins in 1982.)

For several reasons, the field-goal holder on many teams is a quarterback. One of the reasons is that quarterbacks are sure-handed. Another is that going back to high school and college days, they traditionally hold for kickers.

But the best reason is that they can pick up an errant snap and do something with the ball or their teams can set up the fake and have a professional passer ready to pull off the play.

Jim Zorn, a quarterback and kick-holder for the Seattle Seahawks, tossed a 23-yard pass to Theotis Brown for a touchdown in his team's 23-21 loss to the Houston Oilers. Guido Merkens, a backup quarterback and wide receiver who holds for the Saints, threw a 15-yard scoring pass to Wayne Wilson on another fake field-goal attempt in New Orleans's 27-17 victory over the Kansas City Chiefs.

And the most dangerous holder, Nolan Cromwell of the Los Angeles Rams, scored his third career touchdown on a field-goal attempt when he dashed 17 yards against the Denver Broncos in a 1982 game. Though Cromwell is the team's all-pro safety, he was a running quarterback at the University of Kansas.

Even in the strange short season, more teams were getting a kick out of their would-be kicking plays.

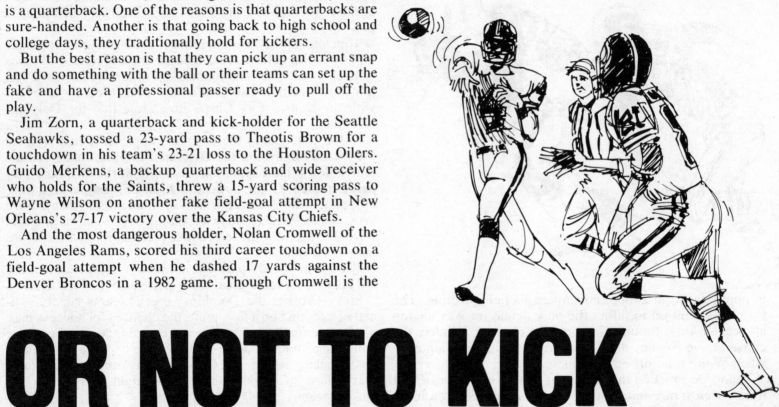

OR NOT TO KICK

When Chuck Knox took over as head coach of the Seattle Seahawks after the 1982 season, he, as so many coaches do, brought in his own cadre of assistants. However, he retained one assistant from the previous staff, Rusty Tillman. As special-teams coach, Tillman had built a reputation for designing fake-kick plays. With Jim Zorn, the team's quarterback, as the holder on field-goal attempts, the Seahawks have had an extra weapon on the field for kicks.

But the Seahawk plays are not just designed for Zorn (H-holder) to take a snap and stand up or drop back to pass. The plays are much more innovative than that.

On this play, Zorn settles into his usual holder's position and two ends (R-receiver) and two wingbacks (R) take the standard protect-the-kicker positions. Should a pass be thrown from holder Zorn, these four players are the targets. But not for the Seahawks. On this play, Zorn flips the ball to Norm Johnson (K), a pretty good athlete in his own right. As the receivers spread out in the pattern shown, opening up the heart of the defense, Zorn meanders into the middle of the line and Johnson tosses back to Zorn.

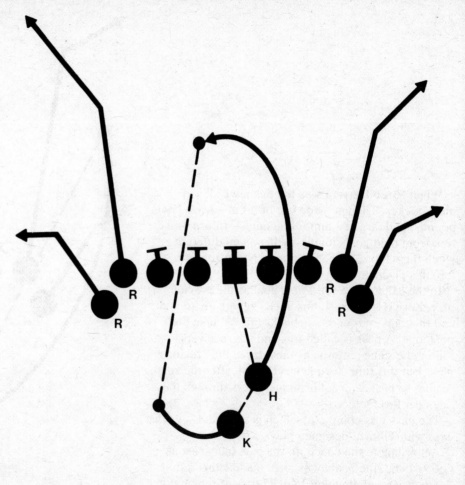

When Efren Herrera was the Seahawk place-kicker, Tillman made use of his good size (190 pounds) and targeted him for a couple of Zorn passes, too, from field-goal situations. It was no different when the 6 foot 2 inch, 193-pound Norm Johnson took his place in 1982.

In the exact setup for a field goal as the previous play, Zorn (H) holds, Johnson (K) gets ready to kick, and the tight ends and wingbacks (all Rs) take their positions. A pass is called for, and the receivers follow the same patterns as they did in the previous play. But this time Zorn keeps the ball after the snap, readies to pass, and Johnson meanders through the line near the center.

The pass was complete, which is almost always the case with Tillman-designed plays.

According to the coach, in the past four seasons (1979–1982), the Seahawks have made either a first down or a touchdown on 15 of 17 tries at running or passing on field-goal situations.

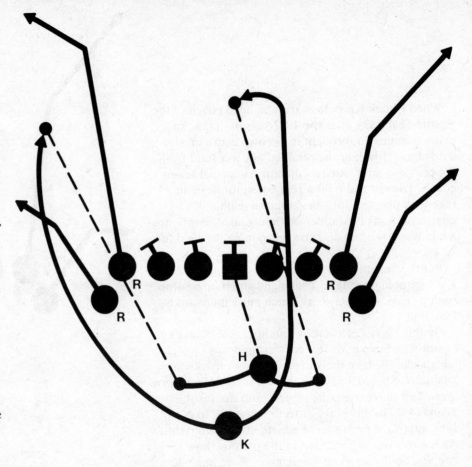

THIRD QUARTER

THE CONFERENCE CHAMPIONSHIP GAMES

3RD QUARTER

With the San Francisco 49ers not even making the NFC playoffs and the New York Jets stunning the Cincinnati Bengals in the first round of the AFC playoffs in "the Super Bowl Tournament," the way was open to the Rose Bowl in Pasadena, California, for two fresh sets of faces in Super Bowl XVII.

It all came down to two interesting match-ups: the Jets versus the Miami Dolphins for the AFC title and the Washington Redskins versus the Dallas Cowboys for the NFC championship.

The Jets had not been in a conference title game since the 1968 season, when they were still playing under the auspices of the American Football League (AFL) and went on to win Super Bowl III. The Dolphins had not been back to the AFC title game since the 1973 season, when their Super Bowl string ran out.

The Redskins' first and only conference playoff game for a title since the early 1940s had been a decade before. Only the Cowboys, a perennial playoff power, were staffed with championshiplike veterans.

Thus the final four came into the conference championships full of new ideas, counting the veteran Cowboys, who have always been pro-football innovators.

On the following pages, some of the key plays of those two crucial championship games are replayed.

THE CHAMPIONSHIPS

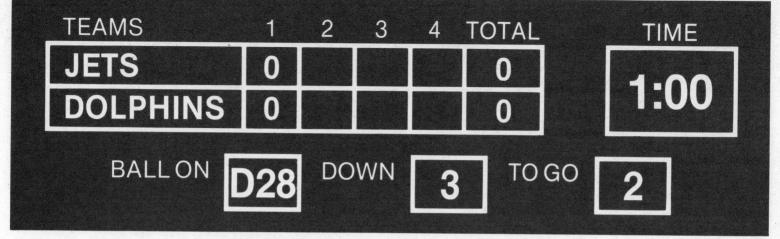

TEAMS	1	2	3	4	TOTAL	TIME
JETS	0				0	1:00
DOLPHINS	0				0	

BALL ON **D28**   DOWN **3**   TO GO **2**

THE SITUATION In this championship game, controversy reigned because of the rain: the home-team Dolphins had not put a tarp on their grass field despite the constant downpour during the week. Now, in the soaking first half, with the field spongy from the rain, neither team was having much success moving the ball. After a 6-yard run by Andra Franklin and 2 more yards after a pitchout to Tony Nathan, the smaller running back, the Dolphins have a small drive mounted. David Woodley, the quarterback, has had good success in playoff games to date, but this weather is not geared to pinpoint passing, especially against a defensive charge like the Jets'. At this juncture, it looked as if breaks between the two powerful defensive teams would be factors. Yet Miami must control the ball.

What should the Dolphins do?

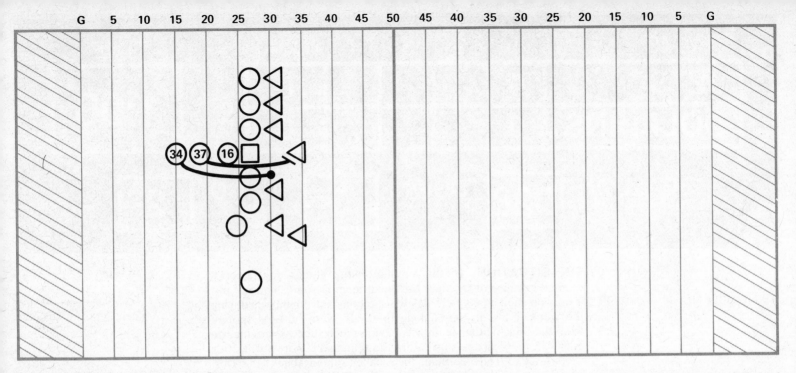

THE DECISION The Dolphins stack their offense in a straight power formation, with Woody Bennett (34) filling in for Nathan and being the deep man, right behind the other runner, Franklin (37). This is called the Dolphins' "Elephant Backfield," and it's geared for tough, straight-ahead yardage. No use going for the fancy cuts on such soggy ground. Woodley (16) calls for a straight handoff to Bennett after Franklin leads him through the hole over the strong-side right guard.

THE RESULT Franklin cleared the hole, and Bennett followed him through, but that was about all. The Dolphins were stopped for a 1-yard gain and were forced into a punting situation.

152

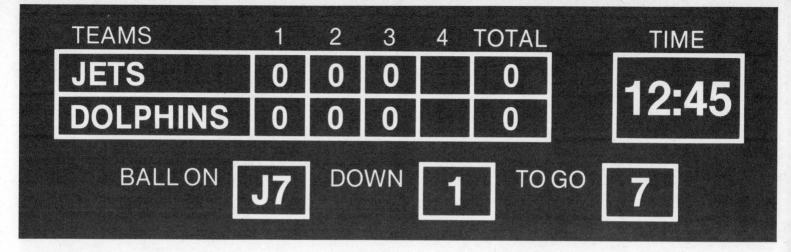

TEAMS	1	2	3	4	TOTAL	TIME
JETS	0	0	0		0	12:45
DOLPHINS	0	0	0		0	

BALL ON **J7** DOWN **1** TO GO **7**

THE SITUATION After the scoreless first half in which the Dolphins did not get any closer than the Jets' 45-yard line, they are rolling after an interception by A. J. Duhe on the Jets' 48. Both the running and passing games are working for Miami, which twice made first downs on third-down plays. One of them was a pass from Woodley to Duriel Harris for 14 yards.

With the ball on the Jets' 7 and the weather letting up somewhat, the Dolphins are finally within scoring range. Woodley's passing has not been sharp all day, and most of his completions have been short stuff to the running backs. But the running game has not been very effective, either, on this field. The Jets may be down a bit because after Harris's catch to the Jets' 14, an unsportsmanlike-conduct call has moved the ball to the 7-yard line.

The Dolphins have been getting the breaks, with the interception and the penalty, but now it is up to them to create some activity of their own in deep scoring territory and four downs to go.

Keep in mind that the Dolphins, at this point in the game, do not know what kind of shape their field-goal kicker, Uwe von Schamann is in; he is coming off a back injury. Thus, the touchdown is much more desirable.

Lots of options on this play, but which one is best?

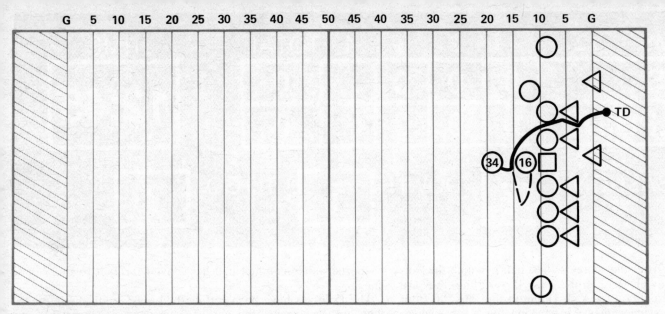

THE DECISION   Woodley (16) has his receivers split wide, able to go to the corners or work the flanks in any of several ways. Only one big back, Bennett (34), is deep in the backfield, giving him another back up near the line for a short pass or blocking to the left. The call is for Woodley to roll out slightly to the right, then hand off to Bennett for a power play over the left guard. It doesn't seem like a play designed for a touchdown from so far out, but the Jet defense is forced to spread out because of the many options, including a Woodley rollout pass or run to the right.

THE RESULT   A tough, powering run by Bennett. He bulled his way to, and just over, the goal line after struggling to make his first few yards. The Dolphins had the first score of the game.

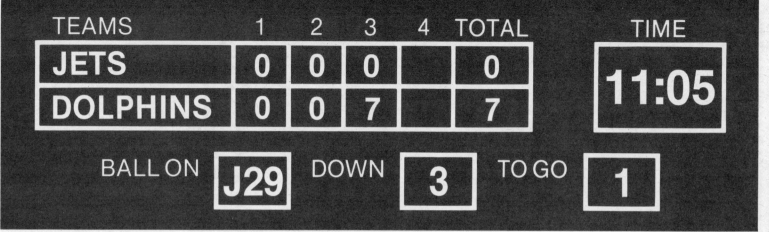

TEAMS	1	2	3	4	TOTAL	TIME
JETS	0	0	0		0	11:05
DOLPHINS	0	0	7		7	

BALL ON **J29** DOWN **3** TO GO **1**

THE SITUATION Richard Todd, the Jets' quarterback, is having even more problems than his Miami counterpart, Woodley: sacks, interceptions, inability to spring loose his receivers. Freeman McNeil, the league's leading rusher, is going nowhere on a field where he cannot cut on his sweeps. He has slipped a couple of times trying to push his outside foot into the spongy field. Lam Jones and Wesley Walker, the outstanding long receivers, just are not in synch with Todd. The other running backs, Mike Augustyniak and Scott Dierking, have been held in check, hardly even being utilized.

But a first down will keep the drive going on this first series following the Miami touchdown.

How do you keep the drive alive?

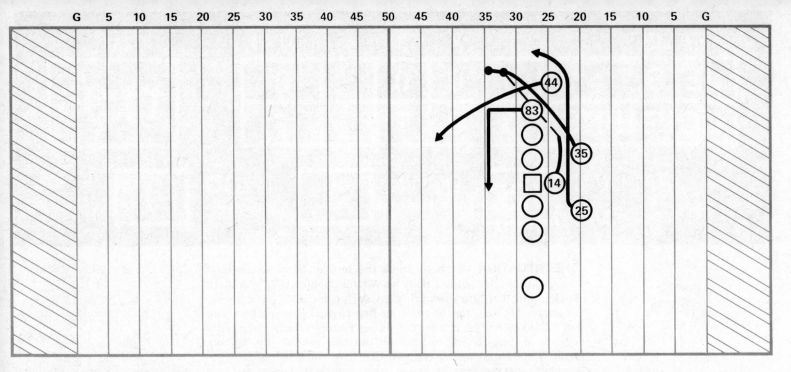

THE DECISION Richard Todd (14) has a full backfield full of runners and short-yardage receivers. Scott Dierking (25) and Mike Augustyniak (35) are the deep backs, and Tom Newton (44), a fullback, is set in a wingbacklike position, just behind and to the right of Jerome Barkum (83), the tight end.

Because Miami puts only four men up on the line at first, a pass might be suspected. Todd's call is for Dierking to go to the right, parallel to the scrimmage line, but for Todd to dump a short pass to Augustyniak, who veers off to the hole between Barkum and Newton.

THE RESULT A successful short-yardage play that got the first down. Augustyniak took the quick pass on the congested right side and lugged it another yard or so for a 3-yard gain.

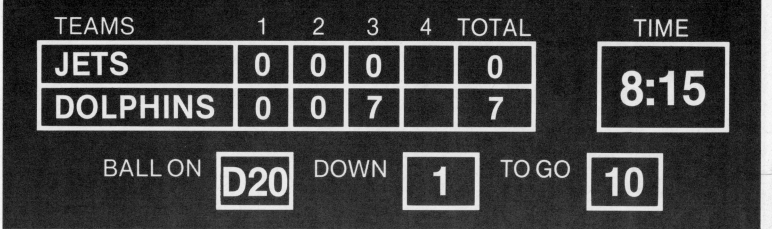

TEAMS	1	2	3	4	TOTAL	TIME
JETS	0	0	0		0	8:15
DOLPHINS	0	0	7		7	

BALL ON **D20**   DOWN **1**   TO GO **10**

THE SITUATION With the weather having let up but the field still a quagmire, it is still anyone's game, and the Dolphins have yet to show they can launch a long drive from so deep in their own territory. Certainly, a 7–0 score has not won a playoff game in well over a decade. The Dolphin runners are not eating up much yardage, and with it much time, and the passing game has not been good.

But here on their own 20, the Dolphins still need to get something moving, or they could lose the ball to the Jets around midfield on a punt.

The Dolphins will line up in a very normal offense, two receivers split wide, two deep backs, and the tight end to the strong side right.

What is the call?

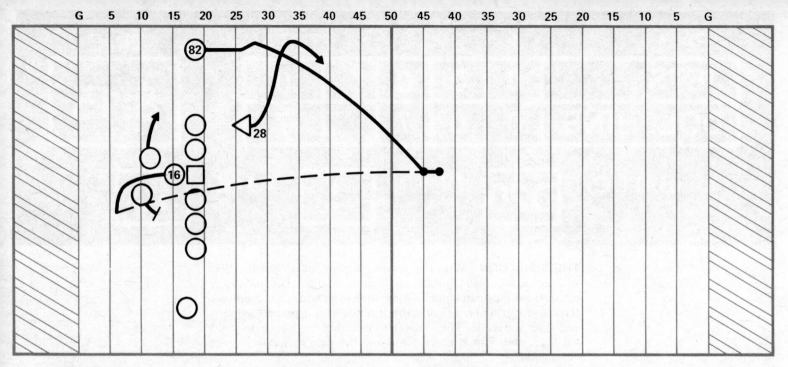

THE DECISION Offensive receivers still have the edge over defensive backs on bad fields; thus, David Woodley (16) went for the straight, drop-back bomb. Duriel Harris (82), the receiver to the left, was his target, and Woodley made an outstanding throw of about 50 yards to Harris, heading to the center of the field, past the 50-yard line.

THE RESULT A Jets defensive free safety, Darrol Ray (28), read the play all wrong, figuring Harris to go to the outside. Ray was pretty much out of the play when Woodley's pass zoomed downfield into Jet territory. Harris had a hand on the ball and couldn't hold it. It was close to a touchdown but ended up an incompletion. Good call, good pass.

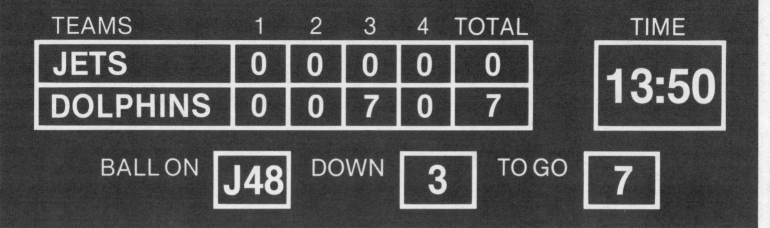

TEAMS	1	2	3	4	TOTAL
JETS	0	0	0	0	0
DOLPHINS	0	0	7	0	7

TIME **13:50**

BALL ON **J48**   DOWN **3**   TO GO **7**

THE SITUATION The Jets are in trouble as the clock winds down and the offense can't wind up. Wesley Walker, the outstanding receiver, has yet to catch a pass. Lam Jones, the other speedster, has been shut down, too. Freeman McNeil, the star running back, has been having trouble making 3 yards a carry all day long. The tight double coverage on receivers, combined with the sacking and intercepting of Richard Todd, the quarterback, has given Miami a strong edge on defense.

Yet the Jets will have decent field position if they can get the third-and-long yardage play off the ground. With McNeil out and Bruce Harper in, it seems as if it is an obvious passing situation. If so, what kind of a pass do you attempt?

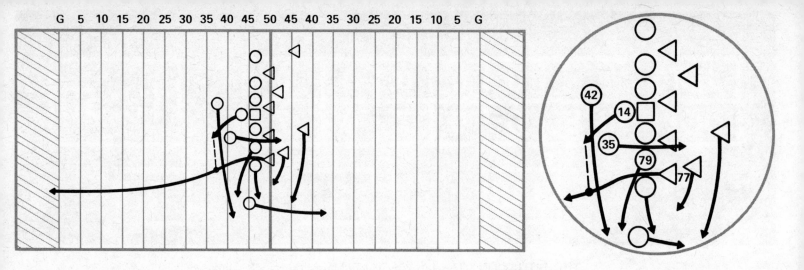

THE DECISION Todd (14) chose to pass to either Bruce Harper (42) in the flat or to Mike Augustyniak (35) over the middle, hoping for a short play that would pick up the 7 yards needed for the first down and at least sustain the drive. Not a bad choice, especially to Harper, because the little back is so effective in an open field. Also, the field conditions would perhaps give him the edge because he is so elusive with cuts and change-up speed that could leave defenders slipping in the mud.

THE RESULT Not the Jets' day at all. Todd rolled back to his right and aimed a pass to Harper, who had moved into the right flat, but in dashed the day's hero, A. J. Duhe (77) of the Dolphins, who had shot through a hole vacated by Marvin Powell (79), who had pulled to block for Harper. Duhe moved into position between Todd and Harper, intercepted, and had a free route to the goal line, 35 yards away.

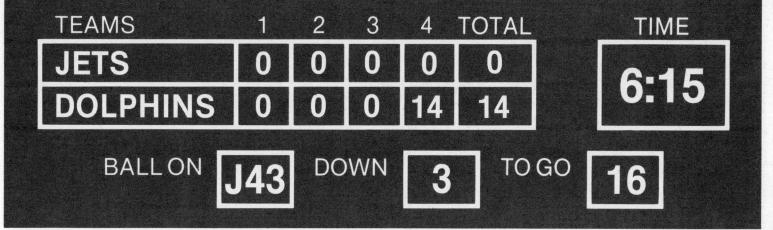

TEAMS	1	2	3	4	TOTAL	TIME
JETS	0	0	0	0	0	6:15
DOLPHINS	0	0	0	14	14	

BALL ON **J43**   DOWN **3**   TO GO **16**

THE SITUATION The Dolphins have the good lead and only need to kill time to earn entry into the Super Bowl. They have the ball, but after David Woodley is sacked, they have the long yardage on third down—and not much hope to avoid a punt. The best they can hope for, it seems, is a long pass or one that will get them into long field-goal range. Woodley goes into the shotgun formation—the Dolphins usually do in this situation.

Considering the conditions, this is a security type of play. What kind of play do you call?

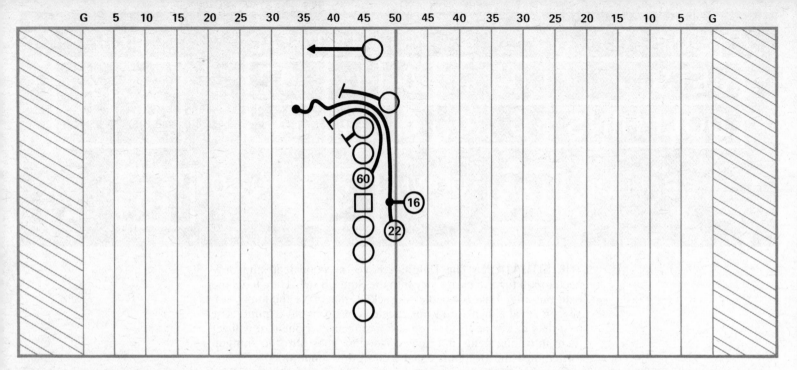

THE DECISION   With his team spread wide for the pass and just one deep back—Tony Nathan (22)—Woodley (16) forgoes the pass and calls instead for a simple running play. In it, he simply hands off to Nathan running right past him after the ball is snapped. Nathan then heads for the right side, trying to pick up the pulling blockers, particularly Jeff Toews (60).

THE RESULT   Not much of anything but a time-killer as the Jets were well protected against a passing situation. The play gained 7 yards of the 16 needed, leaving the Dolphins in a punting situation. The ensuing punt, however, put the Jets in a hole, and they never recovered as the Dolphins earned their way to the Super Bowl.

OFFICIAL TIMEOUT!

FRONT-OFFICE STRATEGY:
THE OL' FIRE–HIRE PLAY

As football teams sat idle during the long 1982 player strike, Jack Patera, the only head coach the Seattle Seahawks ever had, lost his job. Patera was replaced, on an interim basis, by Mike McCormack of the Seahawk front office.

The firing of Patera was not earth shocking by NFL standards. There is an old saying that a coach is hired for one thing (winning) and fired for another (losing), and that it is just a matter of time before the numbers on the right side of the W-L hyphen are bigger than the numbers on the left side.

But in the 1982 season, the pressure on coaches was greater than usual. Including McCormack, who would be replaced after the season, there would be eight more coaching changes besides Patera. The changeovers—not all of which were firings—were epidemic, the most in league history.

But does a coaching change help a team that much?

Of the 20 head coaches who survived the 1982 season and its immediate aftermath, only five had done better than a .500 winning percentage their first year on the job with their current teams. The combined first-year winning percentage was a mere .365. Granted, that percentage was brought down by such coaches as Tom Landry of the Dallas Cowboys, who was 0–11–1 when he began with an expansion team and John McKay, who was 0–14 when he helped begin the Tampa Bay Buccaneer franchise. But some other coaches, who wound up in several Super Bowls—notably Bud Grant of the Minnesota Vikings and Chuck Noll of the Pittsburgh Steelers—had to survive some rocky starts to survive with established teams. Grant's first Viking team was 3–8–3. Noll made his debut by posting a 1–13 mark.

The 1982 Rocky Start Award went to Frank Kush, whose Baltimore team was 0–8–1.

Of those eight franchises that had coaching turnovers after the 1982 season, only the Los Angeles Rams had a coach who was better than .500 in his first season with the franchise (Ray Malavasi, with a 12–4 record).

Malavasi's replacement with the Rams, John Robinson, is just one of seven of the eight new coaches who have never been in charge of an NFL team before. The lone exception is Chuck Knox of the Seahawks, who had a 12–2 record when he debuted with the Rams back in 1973. None of the current 28 coaches was even close to that for his rookie season.

So do you gain anything or not by getting rid of the man at the top? Check the accompanying chart and decide for yourself. Whatever your conclusions, don't expect too much from a new coach.

TEAMS WITH COACHING CHANGES FOR 1983

Team	New Coach	Previous coach and first-year record with team
Atlanta	Dan Henning	Leeman Bennett, 7-7, 1977
Buffalo	Kay Stephenson	Chuck Knox, 5-11, 1978
Kansas City	John Mackovic	Marv Levy, 4-12, 1978
L.A. Rams	John Robinson	Ray Malavasi, 12-4, 1978
N.Y. Giants	Bill Parcells	Ray Perkins, 6-10, 1979
N.Y. Jets	Joe Walton	Walt Michaels, 3-11, 1977
Philadelphia	Marion Campbell	Dick Vermeil, 4-10, 1976
Seattle	Chuck Knox	Jack Patera, 2-12, 1976

VETERAN COACHES

Team	Coach	First-year record with current team
Baltimore	Frank Kush	0-8-1, 1982
Chicago	Mike Ditka	3-6, 1982
Cincinnati	Forrest Gregg	6-10, 1980
Cleveland	Sam Rutigliano	8-8, 1978
Dallas	Tom Landry	0-11-1, 1960
Denver	Dan Reeves	10-6, 1981
Detroit	Monte Clark	7-9, 1978
Green Bay	Bart Starr	4-10, 1975
Houston	Ed Biles	7-9, 1981
L.A. Raiders	Tom Flores	9-7, 1979
Miami	Don Shula	10-4, 1970
Minnesota	Bud Grant	3-8-3, 1967
New England	Ron Meyer	5-4, 1982
New Orleans	Bum Phillips	4-12, 1981
Pittsburgh	Chuck Noll	1-13, 1969
St. Louis	Jim Hanifan	5-11, 1976
San Diego	Don Coryell	8-4, 1978
San Francisco	Bill Walsh	2-14, 1979
Tampa Bay	John McKay	0-14, 1976
Washington	Joe Gibbs	8-8, 1981

Won-loss figures are for regular-season games only.

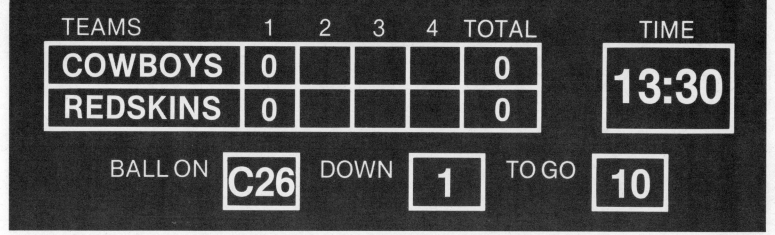

TEAMS	1	2	3	4	TOTAL
COWBOYS	0				0
REDSKINS	0				0

TIME **13:30**

BALL ON **C26** DOWN **1** TO GO **10**

THE SITUATION It is a matchup between the playoff-seasoned Dallas Cowboys and the surprising Washington Redskins, who are trying for their first NFC title since 1972. A coaches' game, too, pairing the innovative newcomer, Joe Gibbs of the Redskins, against the venerable master, Tom Landry of the Cowboys. Dallas was the only team to defeat the Redskins in regular-season play, and they did it convincingly, 24–10. Both teams are at full strength. Washington's Art Monk, a top receiver, is out, but Alvin Garrett has been remarkable as a replacement, neutralizing the loss. Dallas has Ron Springs, its regular fullback, back in the lineup.

Dallas received the kickoff and at this juncture, in its first series, brings the ball to a first down on the Cowboy 26 after a carry by Tony Dorsett and a pass from Danny White to Drew Pearson. The Cowboys, however, are still deep in their own territory and need to gain some ground. How should they do it?

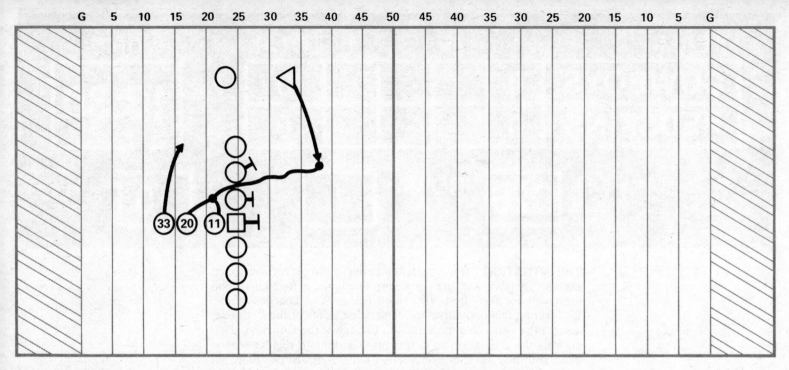

THE DECISION Hit the left side of the line with Ron Springs (20) on a play in which he scored against Washington earlier in the season. Nothing fancy; just try to blow out the Redskins' front line, using Tony Dorsett (33) as a decoy in a pattern where Danny White (11) looks as though he may be faking to Springs and going back for a pass.

THE RESULT A solid 12-yard gain and the knowledge that Springs is back in form after being out.

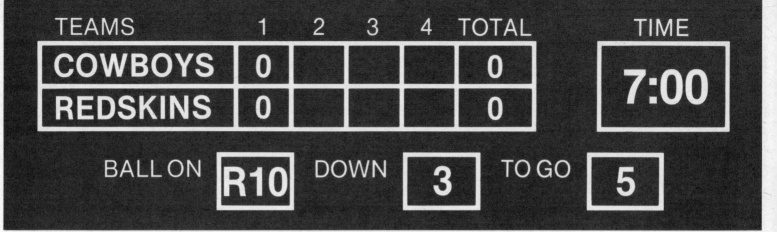

TEAMS	1	2	3	4	TOTAL
COWBOYS	0				0
REDSKINS	0				0

TIME 7:00

BALL ON **R10** DOWN **3** TO GO **5**

THE SITUATION   The Cowboys have moved all the way to the Redskins' 10-yard line on their first possession of the game and are threatening to score. It is a big down, though, if the Cowboys are intent on getting 7 points instead of a field goal. The Cowboys usually go with the two running backs, Tony Dorsett and Ron Springs, down here, so you have to figure Washington must be thinking of the blitz. If you want to pass, it will probably have to be something you can get off quickly. Or do you want to run?

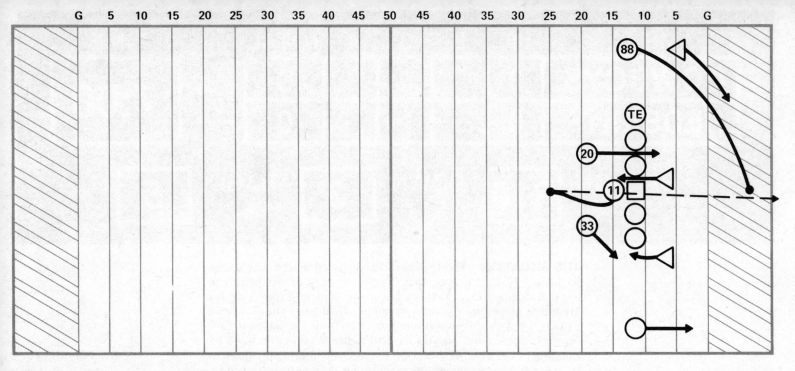

THE DECISION   A quick drop-back by Danny White (11) and a quick pass to Drew Pearson (88) cutting over and going deep into the end zone. Ron Springs (20) and Tony Dorsett (33) are headed down to the goal-line area for a possible first-down catch if Pearson is covered.

THE RESULT   The blitz was on, but Pearson broke away and got to the back of the end zone, only to narrowly miss making the catch. The Cowboys had to settle for the field-goal attempt, which they made to take the early lead.

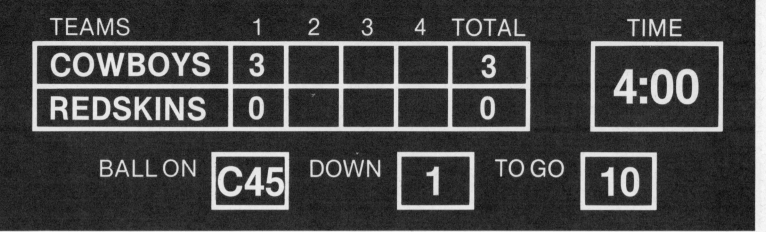

TEAMS	1	2	3	4	TOTAL	TIME
COWBOYS	3				3	4:00
REDSKINS	0				0	

BALL ON **C45** DOWN **1** TO GO **10**

THE SITUATION The Redskins are rolling downfield on their first possession of the game, and this is their sixth play from scrimmage. They have gained 45 yards on three carries by John Riggins, the fullback, and two passes from Joe Theismann to his tight ends. With a first down and 10 at about midfield, this is one of those typical Redskin setup situations in which they have been battering away at you with the routine stuff and then come up with something fancy. But there is no harm staying with the routine, either, when you are making yardage. What do you call?

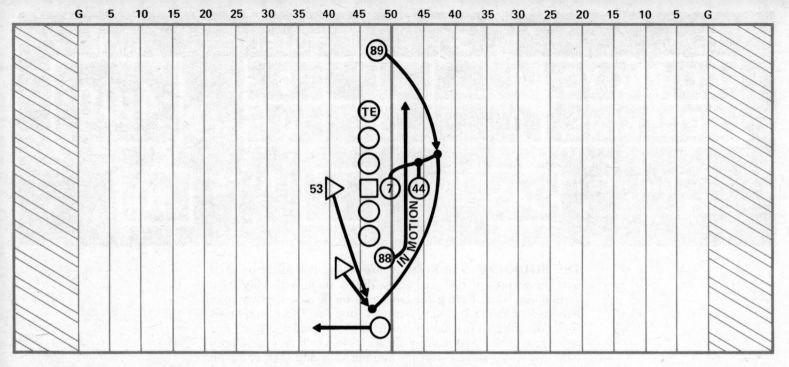

THE DECISION The Redskins get fancy. The play is one in which Joe Theismann (7) hands off to John Riggins (44) again, headed for a hole on the strong side. But Riggins does a quick turn, giving the ball to Alvin Garrett (89). Rick Walker (88) is in motion, coming from the left slot, adding to the confusion for the Cowboys.

THE RESULT The Cowboys read this one and snared Garrett for a 2-yard loss as Bob Breunig (53) followed Garrett almost all the way.

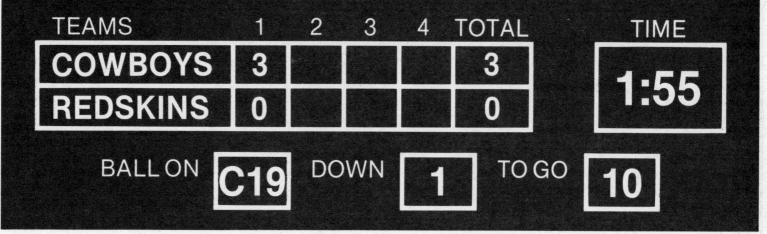

TEAMS	1	2	3	4	TOTAL
COWBOYS	3				3
REDSKINS	0				0

TIME

1:55

BALL ON **C19** DOWN **1** TO GO **10**

THE SITUATION The Redskins keep the ball on the move after the reverse by Alvin Garrett gave them a momentary setback. Joe Theismann came back with a pass right away to Garrett, and Riggins made a big carry to get the Redskins down in scoring territory. The Redskins' pattern thus far has been Riggins, Riggins, Riggins, interspersed with Theismann mixing up his passes. All three pass attempts have been completed, and Riggins already has 32 yards on four carries. Everything is working, so how do you stay hot?

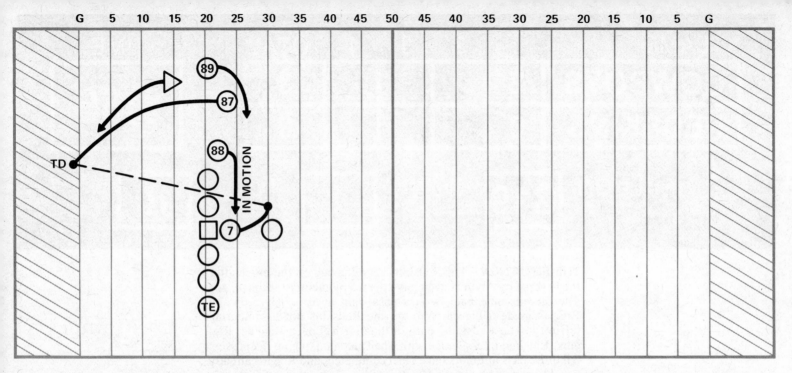

THE DECISION The Redskins have yet to try a long pass and have yet to use Charlie Brown, a fine long receiver. Brown (87) gets the call on a down-and-in pattern. Rick Walker (88) is in motion on the play, and Alvin Garrett (89) comes around from Brown's side to draw attention away from the long receiver.

THE RESULT Joe Theismann (7) was right on the mark, and the Redskins had the first touchdown of the game.

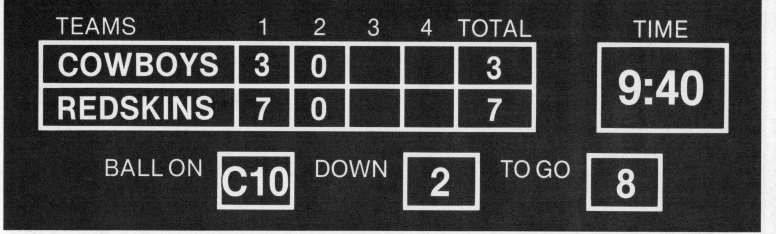

TEAMS	1	2	3	4	TOTAL	TIME
COWBOYS	3	0			3	9:40
REDSKINS	7	0			7	

BALL ON **C10**   DOWN **2**   TO GO **8**

THE SITUATION The Redskins are threatening again, having started on their own 40. After five straight carries by John Riggins, Joe Theismann began mixing up his plays more. Garrett has been the target for four passes on this drive. The previous play was a 2-yard gain by Riggins, and a passing attempt seems to be the call. But what do you want to do?

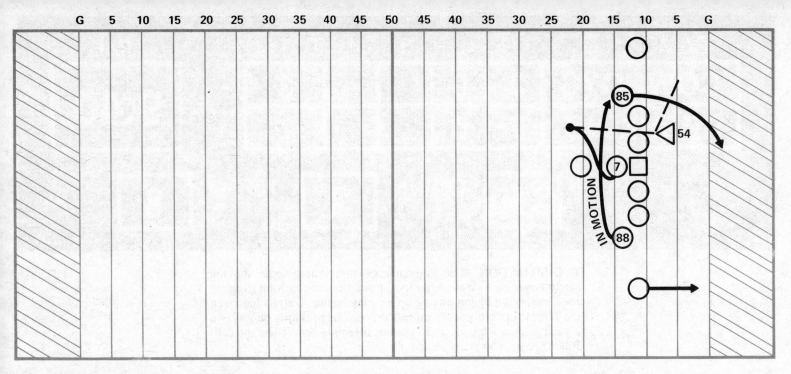

IN MOTION

THE DECISION The Redskins line up for the pass, with their wide receivers split wide on the line and two tight ends, Don Warren (85) and Rick Walker (88), in the backfield. Walker is in motion on this play, but the call is for Warren to take a few steps past the scrimmage line and begin cutting in. Joe Theismann's (7) pass is a quick one to Warren.

THE RESULT The ball was tipped by Randy White (54), the Cowboys' right tackle, as Theismann tried to throw over the tall Dallas line, and the ball fell incomplete. The Redskins eventually had to settle for a field-goal attempt, which failed.

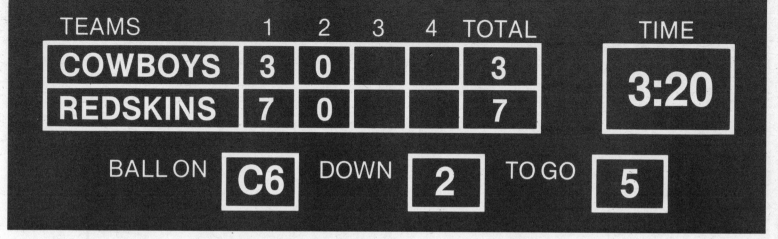

TEAMS	1	2	3	4	TOTAL
COWBOYS	3	0			3
REDSKINS	7	0			7

TIME **3:20**

BALL ON **C6** DOWN **2** TO GO **5**

THE SITUATION The Redskins are down in scoring territory for the third straight time. Their spirits are up, having just recovered a fumble two plays before. They are proving they can move the ball with surprising ease against the Cowboys so far. So what should they do here?

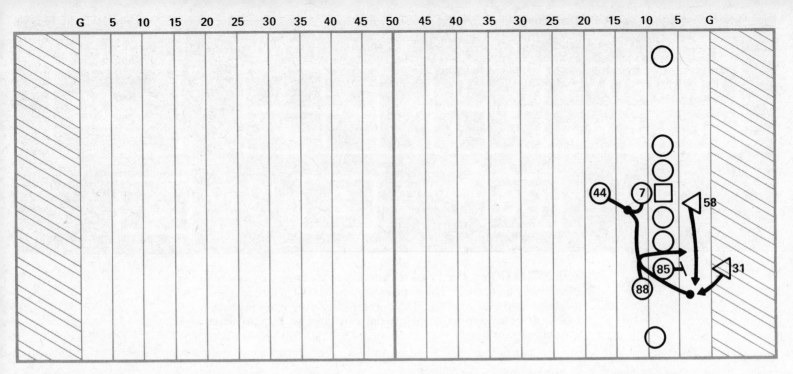

THE DECISION John Riggins (44) gets the ball on a sweep between the two tight ends, Don Warren (85) and Rick Walker (88), who makes the inside block.

THE RESULT Riggins took the handoff from Joe Theismann (7) behind the right guard but didn't have any room to cut in soon and had to go wide. If he has a weakness, it is going laterally instead of powering ahead. Still, he picked up 3 yards before being stopped by Mike Hegman (58) and Benny Barnes (31). Two plays later, Riggins did get to power ahead and got the touchdown.

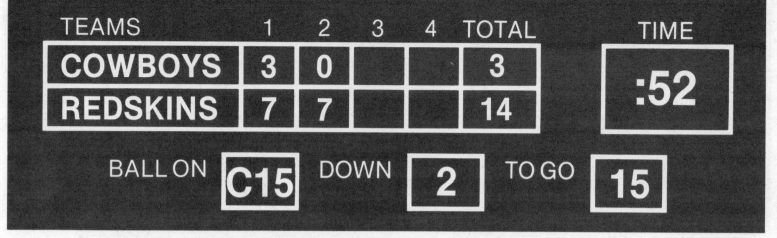

TEAMS	1	2	3	4	TOTAL	TIME
COWBOYS	3	0			3	:52
REDSKINS	7	7			14	

BALL ON **C15** DOWN **2** TO GO **15**

THE SITUATION The Cowboys are getting backed up in this game and need to get the ball moving with time running out in the half. It is a long way to scoring territory, and maybe the best they can hope for is a field goal despite their need for a couple of touchdowns. What do you call?

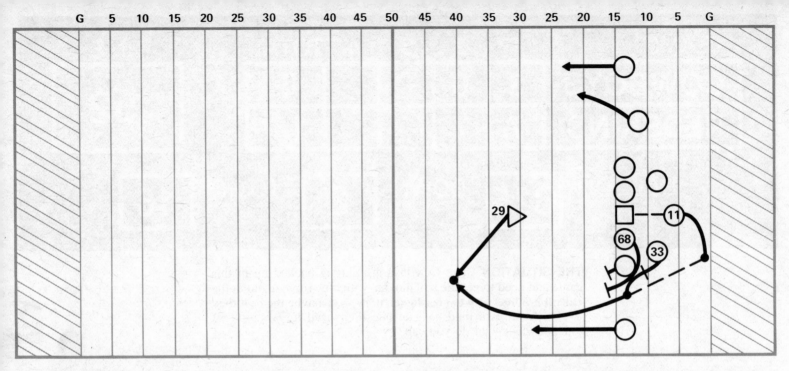

THE DECISION Danny White (11) goes into the shotgun formation. Tony Dorsett's (33) job, with all the receivers split wide, is to fake a little block, then pick up the pulling guard, Herbert Scott (68), and wait for White's screen pass.

THE RESULT A good ground-gainer, for 25 yards, before Mark Murphy (29) of the Redskins finally brought him down. But it was still a long way to scoring territory, and 13 seconds had been used up.

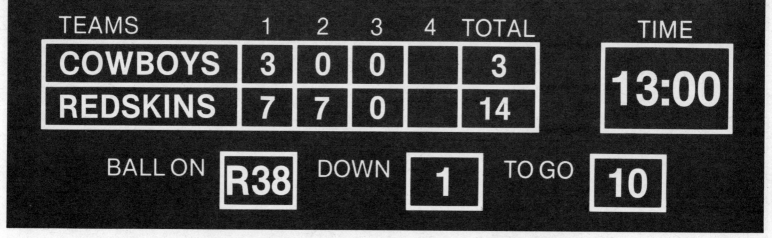

TEAMS	1	2	3	4	TOTAL
COWBOYS	3	0	0		3
REDSKINS	7	7	0		14

TIME **13:00**

BALL ON **R38**   DOWN **1**   TO GO **10**

THE SITUATION   The Cowboys are in trouble early in the second half. They need a couple of touchdowns, and Danny White, their quarterback, is on the bench with an injury he received just before the first half ended. Gary Hogeboom, his replacement, has a great arm, and even though the Cowboys have not used him much during the season, they realize his talent. He threw one pass at the end of the first half and completed it. This is the Cowboys' first play from scrimmage in the second half. Past midfield, they are in good position. What play do you call?

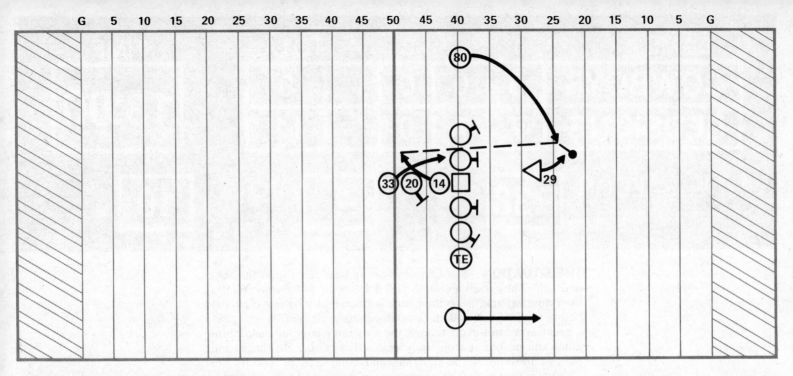

THE DECISION Gary Hogeboom (14), running the team from the I-formation with Ron Springs (20) and Tony Dorsett (33) behind him, goes to Tony Hill (80) on a short down-and-in pass.

THE RESULT A 15-yard completion and a good confidence booster for the young quarterback.

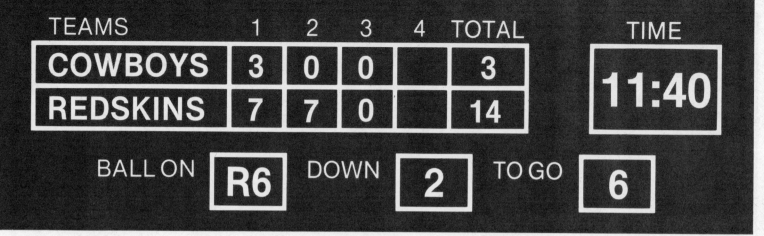

TEAMS	1	2	3	4	TOTAL
COWBOYS	3	0	0		3
REDSKINS	7	7	0		14

TIME

11:40

BALL ON **R6**   DOWN **2**   TO GO **6**

THE SITUATION   Gary Hogeboom has not been afraid to throw, and after four straight passes and a carry by Tony Dorsett, the Cowboys have a chance for a touchdown. The pressure is on the young quarterback, but with good receivers and a running back as good as Dorsett, there are many options on the second-down-and-goal situation. Which option do you like?

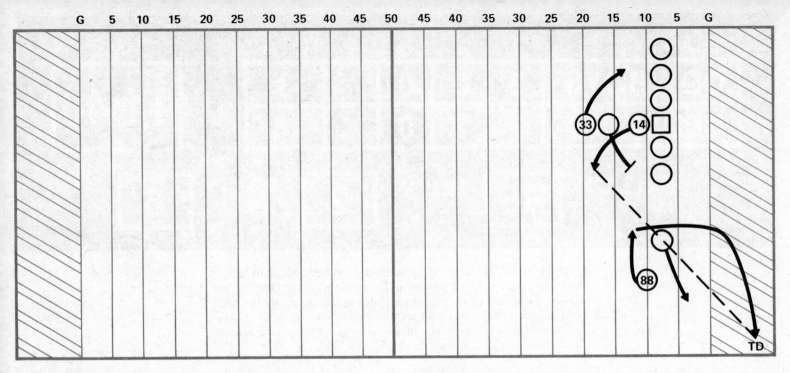

THE DECISION The Cowboys go into the I-formation, with Tony Dorsett (33) the deep back. But the call is for a pass from Gary Hogeboom (14) to Drew Pearson (88) after Pearson goes in motion and then makes a quick cut-in and heads for the sideline in the end zone.

THE RESULT Excellent moves by Pearson and a picture-perfect pass by Hogeboom for the touchdown that put Dallas back in the game.

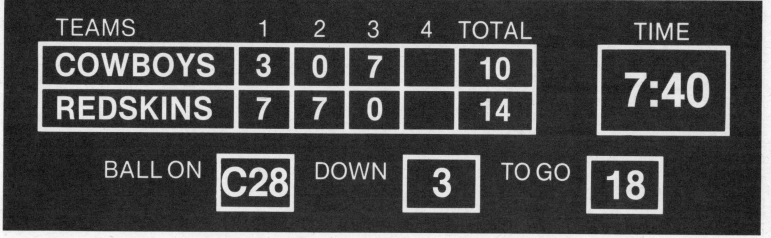

TEAMS	1	2	3	4	TOTAL
COWBOYS	3	0	7		10
REDSKINS	7	7	0		14

TIME 7:40

BALL ON C28   **DOWN** 3   **TO GO** 18

THE SITUATION The Redskins had been having it easy until the Cowboy touchdown pass on the previous series. But the Washington offense has been bogged down in the second half. Mike Nelms's 76-yard kickoff return, however, has made them a threat again, but Joe Theismann and John Riggins and company have got to get something going. Just before this play, Riggins was stopped after a 1-yard gain, and Theismann was sacked for a 9-yard loss. The Redskins are blowing their good field position gained on the Nelms kick return. It's long yardage, and Theismann has to come up with something, even if the Redskins want to salvage a field goal. What should they do?

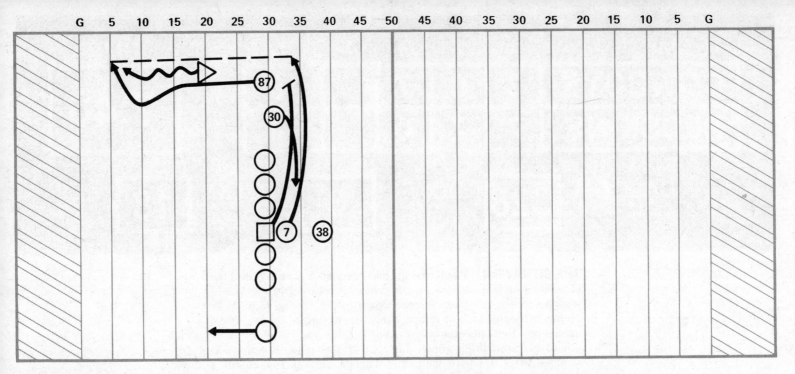

THE DECISION Joe Theismann (7) wants to get the ball to one of his long-gainers, Charlie Brown (87) in this case. The call is for a rollout, with Claude Harmon (38) the deep back and Nick Giaquinto (30) going in motion to the left to draw some pressure off Theismann.

THE RESULT Theismann had to roll out well to the right side, but he eventually found Brown making a good cut to the sideline and completed the pass for 22 yards and a most-important first down. Two plays later, Riggins powered for the touchdown.

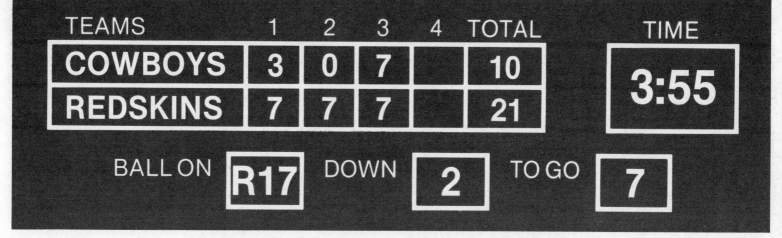

TEAMS	1	2	3	4	TOTAL
COWBOYS	3	0	7		10
REDSKINS	7	7	7		21

TIME

3:55

BALL ON **R17** DOWN **2** TO GO **7**

THE SITUATION Gary Hogeboom has the Cowboys marching to the Redskins' goal line again. He has been hitting on all sorts of passes, and from the shotgun formation alone he is five for five. He has moved the Cowboys from their own 16-yard line. Other than his passing, Tony Dorsett has been carrying the rest of the work load and doing it effectively. This is a big play in light of the Redskins' last touchdown. What do you call?

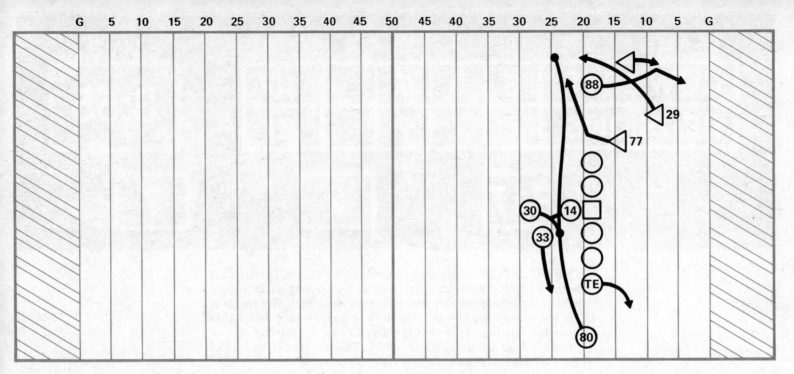

THE DECISION The Cowboys get sneaky. With Timmy Newsome (30) at fullback and Tony Dorsett (33) at the halfback spot, Gary Hogeboom (14) makes a quick pitchout to Newsome, who hands off to Tony Hill (80) coming around on the reverse. Drew Pearson (88) has gone downfield to open up the left side for Hill.

THE RESULT Darryl Grant (77) and Mark Murphy (29) played their areas well on this one and didn't let Hill turn in. Instead, they ganged up on him for a 6-yard loss.

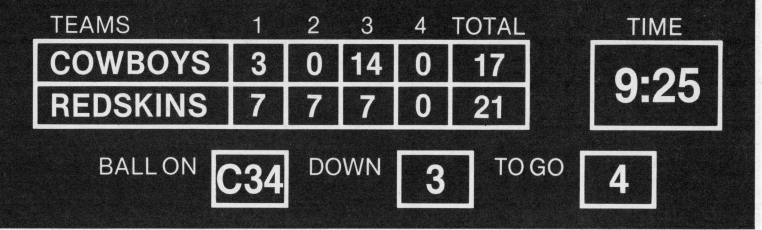

TEAMS	1	2	3	4	TOTAL
COWBOYS	3	0	14	0	17
REDSKINS	7	7	7	0	21

TIME **9:25**

BALL ON **C34**   DOWN **3**   TO GO **4**

THE SITUATION The Cowboys have scored another touchdown and are not about to let the Redskins pull away in this game. There is lots of time left, and the Redskins need to control the ball. John Riggins is not the force he was earlier in the game, and Joe Theismann's passing has tailed off. The Redskins face a situation in which they may have to give up the ball, as they did on the last series, with a punt. The Washington defense is keeping the Redskins in the lead. Time to come up with a first down, or there could be trouble. How do they do it?

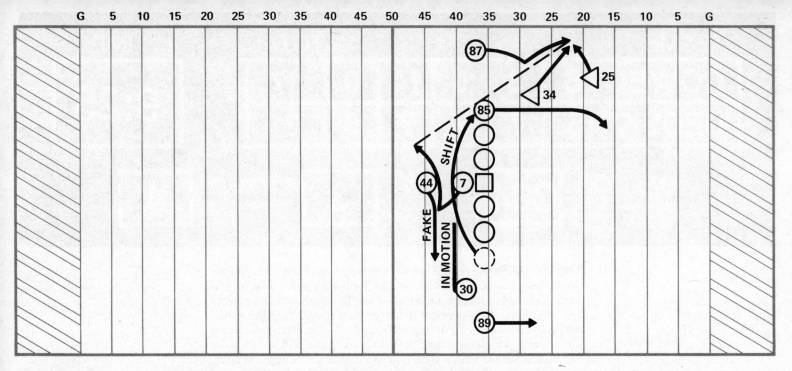

THE DECISION Rather than try to pick away at Dallas, the Redskins go for a big one. Joe Theismann (7) makes the fake to John Riggins (44), which would seem like a natural play to get the first down. Nick Giaquinto (30) is in motion, and Don Warren (85) flipflops from the right tight end to the left side before the snap. Then it is all Theismann to Charlie Brown (87) angling toward the left sideline.

THE RESULT A gutsy call amid all the turmoil and fakery by the Redskins. By the time Rod Hill (25) and Monty Hunter (34) of the Cowboys brought him down, Brown had a 13-yard gain and a much-needed first down. The Redskins went on to score a field goal.

188

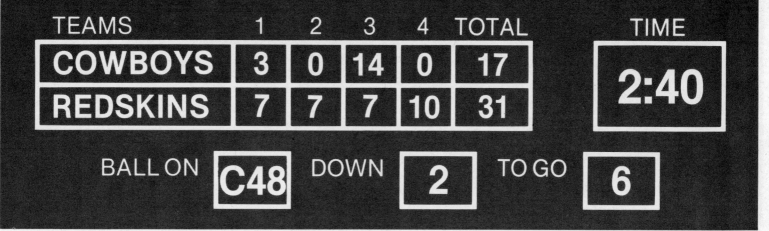

TEAMS	1	2	3	4	TOTAL
COWBOYS	3	0	14	0	17
REDSKINS	7	7	7	10	31

TIME **2:40**

BALL ON **C48**   DOWN **2**   TO GO **6**

THE SITUATION   After another touchdown, all the Redskins had left to do in this game was control the ball as much as possible. That means Riggins, Riggins, Riggins, which is just what the Redskins did on the three previous plays, one of which was good for a first down. Now they need another first down, but not so desperately. How do they get it?

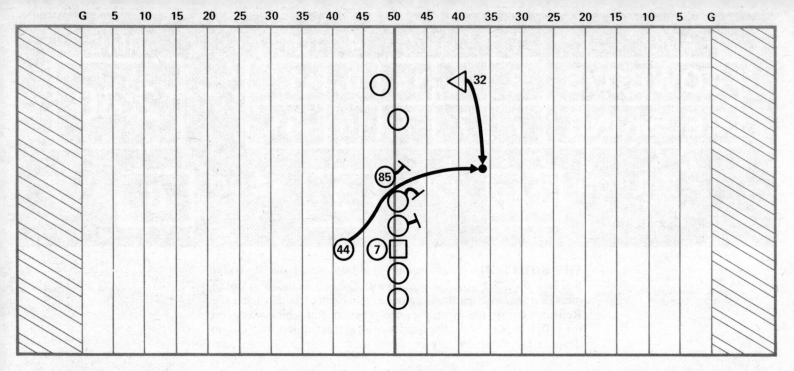

THE DECISION Joe Theismann (7) gives the ball to John Riggins (44). This time, it is to the left side, hoping to pick up a block from Don Warren (85), the tight end.

THE RESULT Riggins did not let the Redskins down. Sprung by Warren's block and then using his own power, he gained 12 yards before Dennis Thurman (32) finally dragged him down. The Redskins continued to eat up the clock and won the game, 31–17.

FOURTH QUARTER

SUPER BOWL XVII

4TH QUARTER

Super Bowl XVII was a matchup of two surprising teams—the Miami Dolphins and the Washington Redskins—but also a testing ground for two of the best coaching staffs to meet in the super game.

Miami had Don Shula, professional football's winningest coach among active coaches.

Washington offered Joe Gibbs, a second-year coach whose Redskin teams had won 19 of 23 previous games.

Among many fine assistants, Shula boasted Bill Arnsparger, his defensive expert, who had put together the toughest defensive team of the 1982 season.

Gibbs had a brilliant top assistant of his own in Dan Henning, who had helped to mold an intricate offense that often utilized three tight ends and more often than not confused many of the league's best defenses as the Redskins compiled an 8–1–0 record before the playoffs.

THE SUPER BOWL

REDSKINS DOLPHINS

It was expected to be a battle of coaching wits as well as talented players. There was no question that strategy was to be the key to Super Bowl XVII, and it turned out that way.

In order to best appreciate one of the finest of all Super Bowls, many of its plays have been recreated on the following pages to allow the reader to study the detailed strategy and to follow how those plays developed.

THE PLAY-BY-PLAY:

The weather at kickoff time at the Rose Bowl was 61 degrees, with just a slight wind and sunny skies. Miami won the coin toss and elected to receive. Mark Moseley kicked off for Washington, and it was returned 17 yards to the Dolphin 25 by Lyle Blackwood.

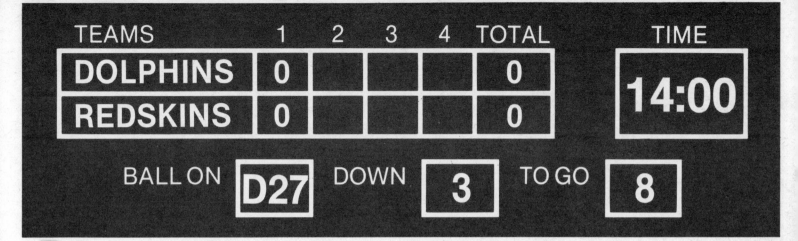

TEAMS	1	2	3	4	TOTAL	TIME
DOLPHINS	0				0	
REDSKINS	0				0	14:00

BALL ON **D27** DOWN **3** TO GO **8**

Dolphins Ball

First and 10/Dolphins' 25: David Woodley's pass to Tony Nathan, incomplete.

Second and 10/Dolphins' 25: Andra Franklin up the middle, 2 yards.

THE SITUATION Long passing yardage is needed for the first down, and in the young game, Woodley has yet to look for one of his long receivers. Jimmy Cefalo and Duriel Harris are his best targets. But both of his backs, Nathan and Franklin, can catch the ball, too.

Who do you go to?

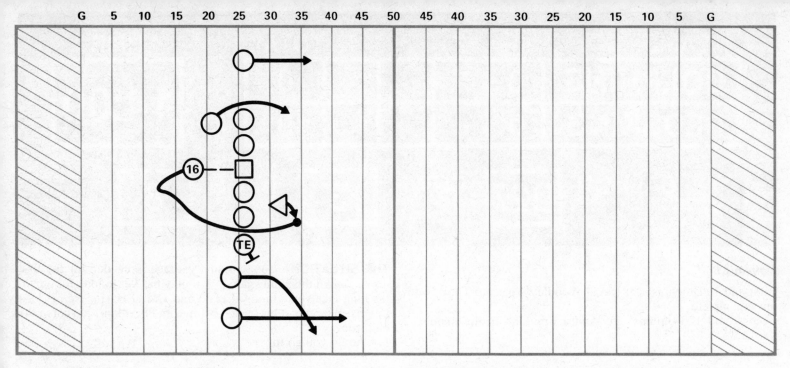

THE DECISION Woodley (16) goes back for the pass, but his receivers are covered. It is hard to tell who his primary receiver is, but all of them except the tight end are headed downfield.

THE RESULT Woodley was forced to scramble, but he picked up a block from the tight end and almost made the first down, coming a yard short.

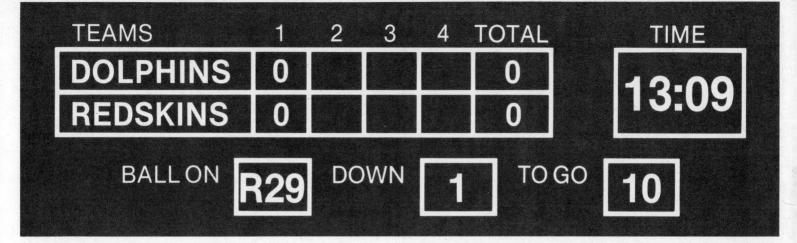

TEAMS	1	2	3	4	TOTAL
DOLPHINS	0				0
REDSKINS	0				0

TIME **13:09**

BALL ON **R29**   DOWN **1**   TO GO **10**

THE PLAY-BY-PLAY

Dolphins' Ball

Fourth and 1/D34: Tom Orosz punts to Redskin 24. Mike Nelms returns it 5 yards to Redskin 29.

THE SITUATION   Washington takes over for its first offensive series of the game. Joe Theismann is the quarterback and has many fine receivers. However, his top receiver for the season, Art Monk, is out of this game with a broken leg. But Alvin Garrett has been sensational as a fill-in, especially in the playoffs. Don Warren is at the tight end, and he is outstanding as a blocker as well as a receiver. Rick Walker is another tight end, often used in the backfield as an extra receiver. John Riggins is the one running back the Redskins go to constantly.

Lots of alternatives on the opening Redskin play. Which one do you choose?

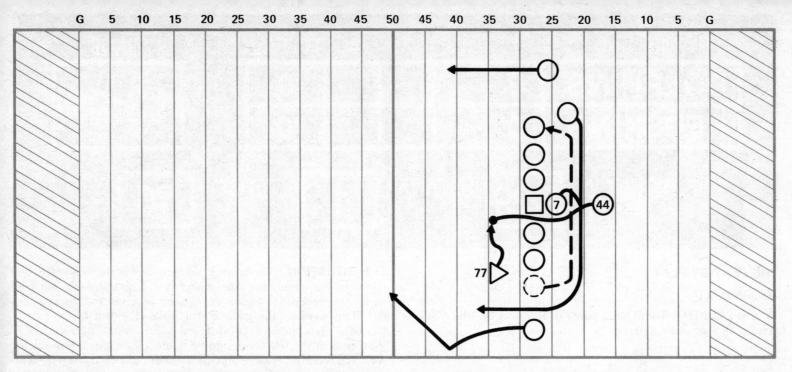

THE DECISION Washington decides to go with its bread-and-butter play—Riggins (44) up the middle. It follows the adage ''Go with your best player on his best play.'' Riggins is at his best when he can drop his shoulders and meet the opposition head-on. If he has a weakness, it is going wide.

THE RESULT Riggins gained 5 yards before A. J. Duhe (77), Miami's standout linebacker, brought him down.

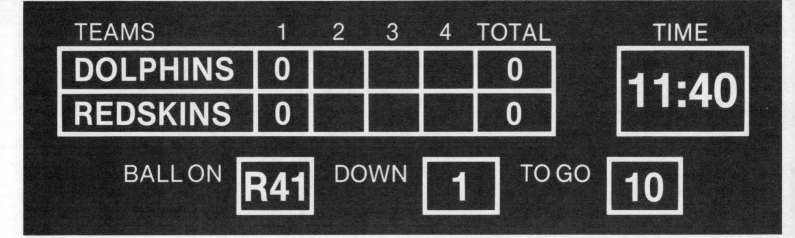

TEAMS	1	2	3	4	TOTAL	TIME
DOLPHINS	0				0	11:40
REDSKINS	0				0	

BALL ON **R41** DOWN **1** TO GO **10**

THE PLAY-BY-PLAY

Redskins' Ball

Second and 5/R34: Riggins over right tackle, 4 yards.
Third and 1/R38: Riggins over right end, 3 yards.

THE SITUATION With first down on their own 41, Washington certainly has established its running game with Riggins. The Redskins have a rule of thumb: if Riggins carries the ball 30 times in a game, they win; if he doesn't, they lose. The system has worked for most of the last two seasons. But Riggins cannot carry the ball the entire 50 or 60 plays that constitute a team's offense. Washington lines up in its standard set: Brown is the flanker in the backfield, and he goes man-in-motion from right to left. Garrett is to the left. Walker, a tight end, is in the backfield. Warren lines up as tight end on the strong side. Should Riggins carry again, or should the Redskins mix it up?

199

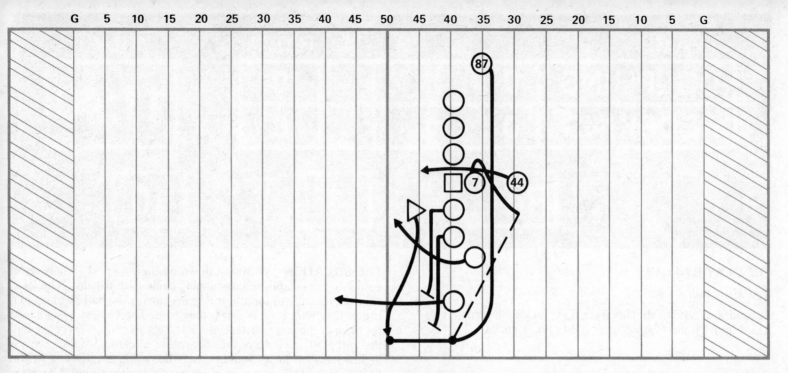

THE DECISION Washington calls for a swing pass to Brown (87), the man-in-motion, who is to catch a short pass and pick up the blocking of the left-side linemen after Theismann (7) fakes a handoff to Riggins (44) going into the right side of the line.

THE RESULT The flanker screen pass to Brown was right on target, and he picked up his blockers to gain 11 yards and Washington's second straight first down.

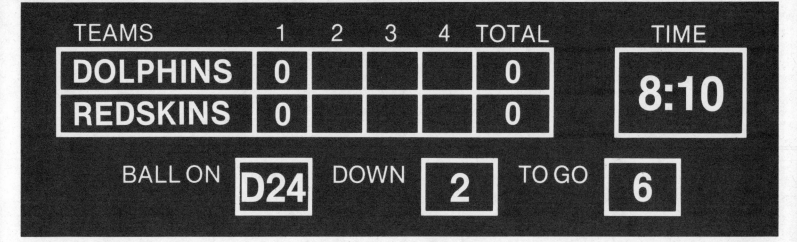

TEAMS	1	2	3	4	TOTAL	TIME
DOLPHINS	0				0	8:10
REDSKINS	0				0	

BALL ON **D24** DOWN **2** TO GO **6**

THE PLAY-BY-PLAY

Redskins' Ball

First and 10/D48: Riggins up the middle, 1 yard.
Second and 9/D47: Theismann's long pass to Garrett, incomplete.
Third and 9/D47: Theismann, back to pass, sacked for 7-yard loss by Earnie Rhone, inside linebacker.
Fourth and 16/R46: Jeff Hayes punt to end zone, no return, 54 yards.

Dolphins' Ball

First and 10/D20: Tony Nathan up the middle, 4 yards.

THE SITUATION

After Miami's first lack of success with the ball, David Woodley, the Dolphin quarterback, has bad field position but is in good shape with Nathan's run. Miami sets up in one of its running sets, Franklin stacked in front of Nathan. It has been said that opponents fear Franklin, the league's number-two rusher, more than faster, elusive Nathan, who carries the ball more loosely. Jimmy Cefalo, split right, is sure-handed but also an elusive receiver. Bruce Hardy is an all-around tight end who goes in motion after setting up to the left. Duriel Harris is a dangerous receiver to the left side and Woodley's favorite wide receiver.

It's anybody's guess. What is yours?

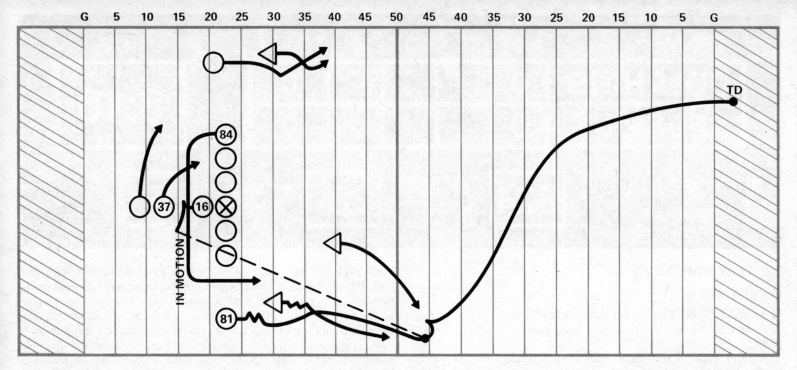

THE DECISION Going off to the left, Woodley (16) decides to fake to Franklin (37) and rolls out slightly to pass to Cefalo (81) on the fly. Woodley has Hardy (84) as outlet man.

THE RESULT Second longest pass in Super Bowl history as Cefalo scampered downfield toward the right sideline, caught a well-thrown pass and outraced the Redskins defense as he cut in toward the middle of the field. Touchdown, Miami! And with it the extra point by Uwe von Schamann and a 7–0 lead.

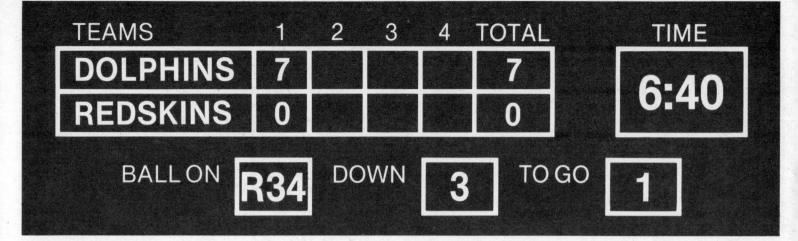

TEAMS	1	2	3	4	TOTAL
DOLPHINS	7				7
REDSKINS	0				0

TIME

6:40

BALL ON **R34**   DOWN **3**   TO GO **1**

THE PLAY-BY-PLAY

Von Schamann kicks off for Dolphins to the Redskin 11, where it is returned by Nelms for 24 yards to the Redskin 35. But a Redskin penalty moves the ball back to their own 25-yard line.

Redskins' Ball

First and 10/R25: Riggins up the middle, 4 yards.
Second and 6/R29: Riggins up the middle, 5 yards.

THE SITUATION

With third down and 1 yard to go, the Redskins' lineup in the usual setup, with Theismann over center and Riggins the deep man. Garrett is split right; Brown is the wide receiver to the left. Walker, a tight end, is in the backfield, to the left of the left tackle. Warren is the tight end, who lines up right but goes in motion to the left. He passes Theismann as the ball is snapped. It's a short-yardage situation, and you are in your own territory. Make your call.

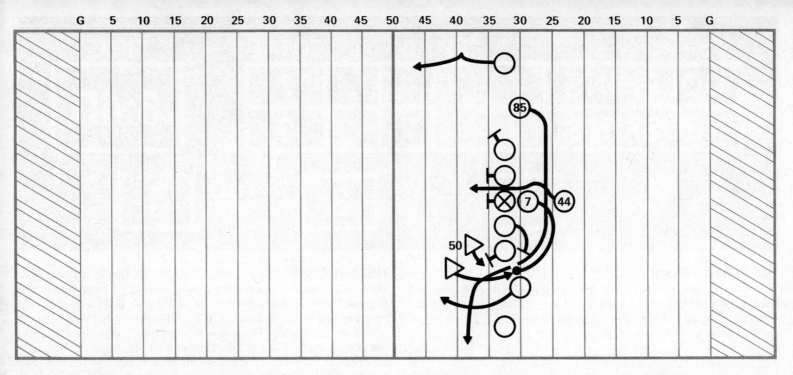

| G | 5 | 10 | 15 | 20 | 25 | 30 | 35 | 40 | 45 | 50 | 45 | 40 | 35 | 30 | 25 | 20 | 15 | 10 | 5 | G |

THE DECISION Theismann (7) calls for a fake to Riggins (44) and a roll to the left to pass. The left guard is to drop back to block for him, freeing Warren (85) to continue the trek around left tackle and into Redskin territory. There are several passing options, with the left side open for Warren and others.

THE RESULT A well-read play as Miami's right linebacker, Larry Gordon (50), broke through for a 3-yard sack.

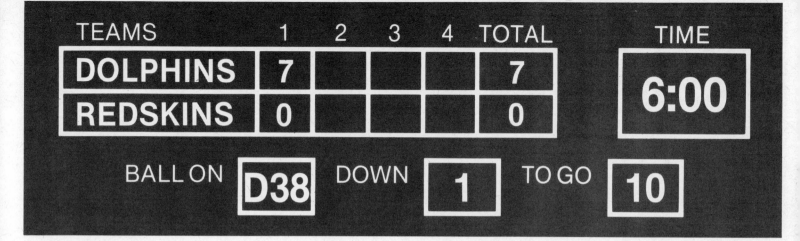

TEAMS	1	2	3	4	TOTAL
DOLPHINS	7				7
REDSKINS	0				0

TIME **6:00**

BALL ON **D38**   DOWN **1**   TO GO **10**

THE PLAY-BY-PLAY

Redskins' Ball

Fourth and 4/R31: Hayes punts to Dolphin 28. Tom Vigorito returns it 10 yards.

THE SITUATION   The Dolphins take over, and it's anybody's guess what kind of play Miami will use in this situation. The Dolphins are chesty after a touchdown pass to Cefalo, and another good pass would establish that part of the Miami game, which is not the team's strong point when Woodley is at quarterback. The heart of the Dolphins' offensive line—Dwight Stephenson at center, Bob Kuechenberg at left guard, and Jeff Toews at right guard—has been looking super on both the pass and the run. Do you stay with the run or try something different to get down deeper in Redskin territory?

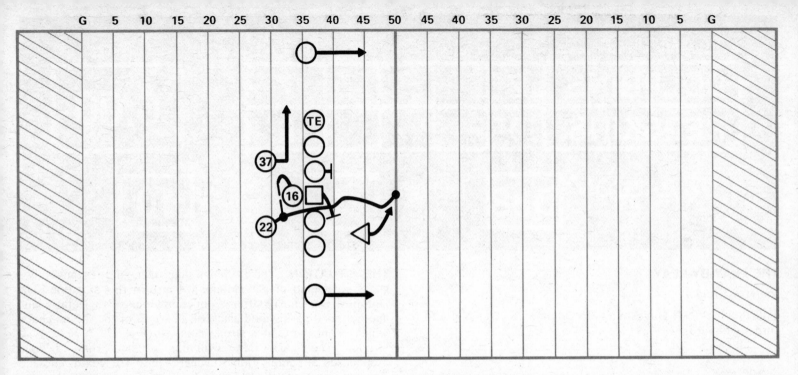

THE DECISION A handoff to Tony Nathan (22) going between guard and center was the call. Andra Franklin (37) is going out of the backfield, over in passing territory on the left flat. The other receivers are headed downfield.

THE RESULT Nathan, helped by Stephenson's block, made a good move into the line, then made a nice cut and went 12 yards for a first down.

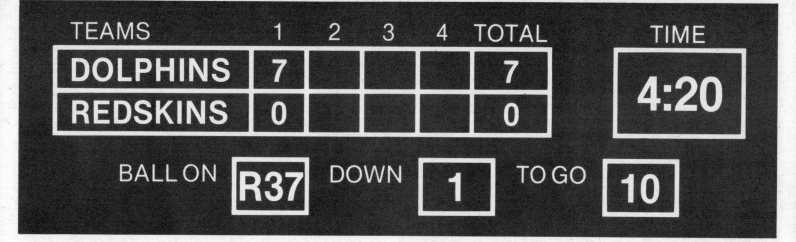

TEAMS	1	2	3	4	TOTAL	TIME
DOLPHINS	7				7	4:20
REDSKINS	0				0	

BALL ON **R37** DOWN **1** TO GO **10**

THE PLAY-BY-PLAY

Dolphins' Ball

First and 10/50: Franklin up the middle, 9 yards.
Second and 1/R41: Franklin up the middle, 4 yards.

THE SITUATION   The Dolphins are on the move with their running game and have a first down on the Redskins' 37-yard line. Again, it is a good opportunity to come up with a variety of plays or even stick with the running game.

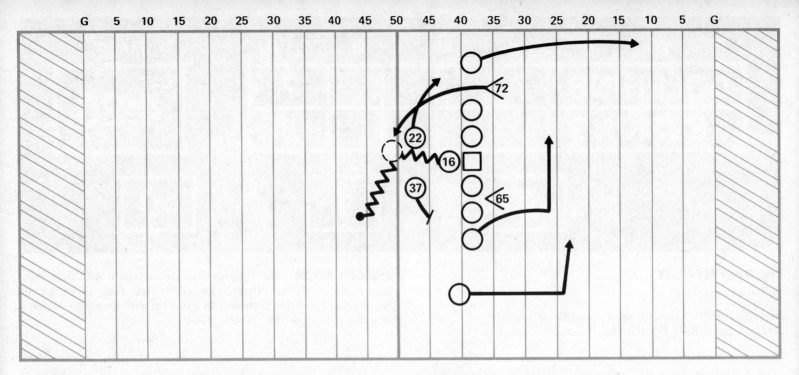

THE DECISION David Woodley (16) drops back to pass in the pocket with Tony Nathan (22) shooting around the left side and Andra Franklin (37) staying back to block. Lots of receivers downfield.

THE RESULT Woodley was hit hard in the pocket by Dexter Manley (72), the Redskins' right end, who forced the fumble. Dave Butz (65), a Redskin tackle, came through and picked up the ball, making it a turnover and a 17-yard loss.

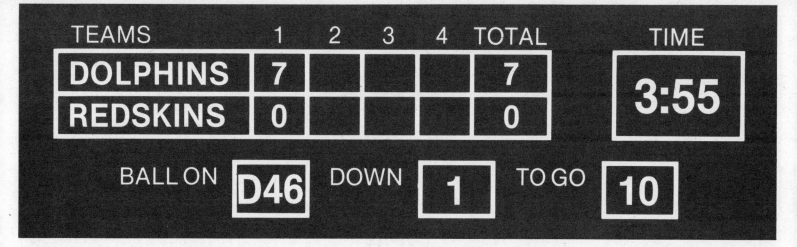

TEAMS	1	2	3	4	TOTAL	TIME
DOLPHINS	7				7	3:55
REDSKINS	0				0	

BALL ON **D46**   DOWN **1**   TO GO **10**

THE PLAY-BY-PLAY

Redskins' Ball

The Redskins take over the ball on the Dolphin 46 after the fumble.

THE SITUATION

The Redskins are down by 7 points, but spirits are up after the fumble recovery in Dolphin territory. Like all situations at this yardline, the options are open. Which one do you choose?

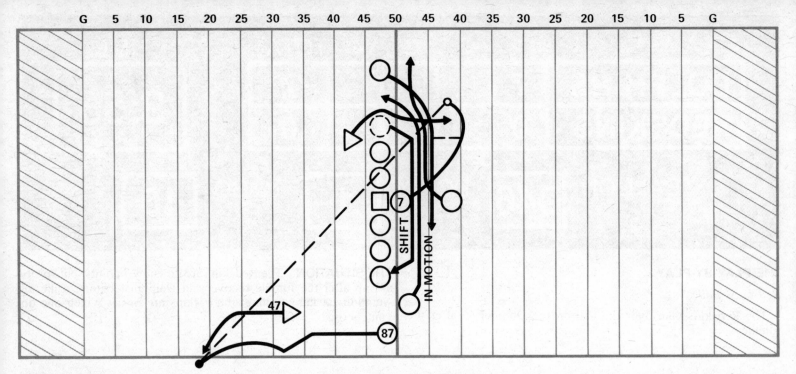

THE DECISION The Redskins call one of their "turmoil" plays, where all sorts of backs, tight ends, and receivers are moving in many directions. Anything can come out of the chaos, which often frees a passer and confuses the opponents, especially on the line and in the backfield. On this play in particular, Joe Theismann (7) drops behind all the movement and lofts a pass to Charlie Brown (87), coming from the left flank.

THE RESULT Brown made a nice catch, but good coverage by Glen Blackwood (47) made him catch it out of bounds.

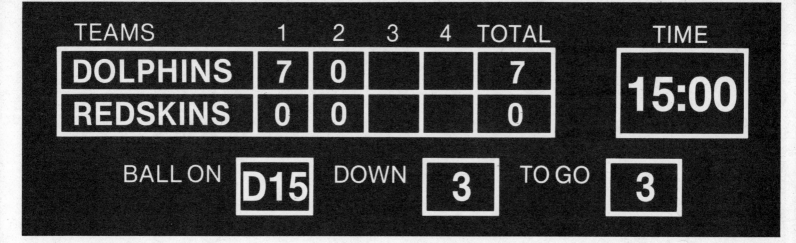

TEAMS	1	2	3	4	TOTAL	TIME
DOLPHINS	7	0			7	**15:00**
REDSKINS	0	0			0	

BALL ON **D15**   DOWN **3**   TO GO **3**

THE PLAY-BY-PLAY

Redskins' Ball

Second and 10/D46: Clarence Harmon over left tackle, 8 yards.
Third and 10/D38: Theismann pass to Warren, 3 yards.
First and 10/D35: Riggins over left tackle, 6 yards.
Second and 4/D29: Riggins at left guard, 7 yards.
First and 10/D22: Riggins over left tackle, 4 yards.
Second and 6/D18: Riggins over left tackle, 3 yards. End of the first quarter.

THE SITUATION   With drives by Riggins, the Redskins are on the Dolphins' 15-yard line and threatening. It is third down and 3 yards to go. Do you stay with Riggins on the carry or try something different?

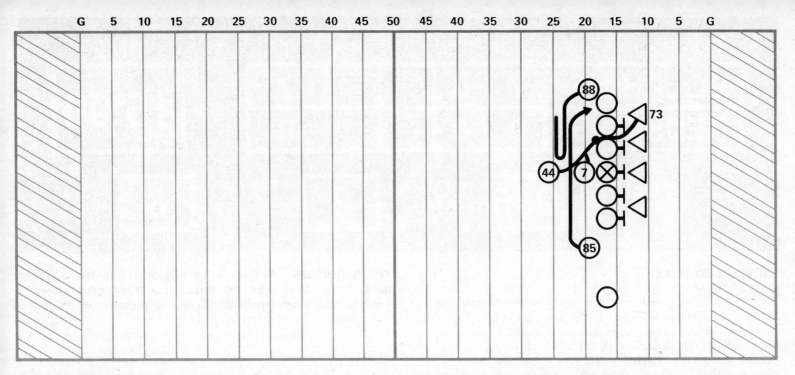

THE DECISION The Redskins choose to go with Riggins (44) over the left tackle. To create some confusion, however, Warren (85) moves from the backfield slot on the right to the left tight end, and Walker (88), a tight end, who is also in the backfield to the left, goes in motion toward Theismann (7), then reverses and goes back to the left to aid Riggins.

THE RESULT Riggins was stopped about 1½ yards short of the first down by Bob Baumhower (73), a defensive tackle, with some help by the rest of the Dolphins. The Redskins were forced into a field-goal-kicking situation instead of a tying touchdown. Mark Moseley made the 31-yard field goal, to close the score to 7–3, Dolphins.

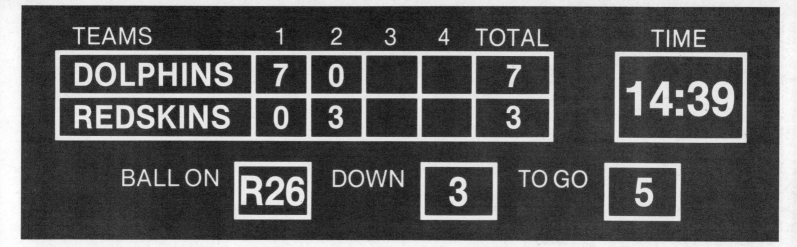

TEAMS	1	2	3	4	TOTAL
DOLPHINS	7	0			7
REDSKINS	0	3			3

TIME

14:39

BALL ON **R26**   DOWN **3**   TO GO **5**

THE PLAY-BY-PLAY

Hayes kicks off after the field goal, and Fulton Walker of the Dolphins returns it 42 yards from the 5- to the 47-yard line.

Dolphins' Ball

First and 10/D47: Nathan takes pitchout around right end, 8 yards.
Second and 2/R45: Nathan up the middle, 3 yards.
First and 10/R42: Franklin slants into the middle, 1 yard.
Second and 9/R41: Woodley's pass to Harris, complete, 8 yards.
Third and 1/R33: Franklin over right guard, 2 yards.
First and 10/R31: Woodley's sideline pass to Cefalo, complete, 6 yards.
Second and 4/R25: Nathan up the middle, loses 1 yard.

THE SITUATION

It is third and 5 on the Redskins' 26, and despite Nathan's 1-yard loss, the first time the Dolphins have lost yardage on a running play all day, the Dolphins are on the move. This is their deepest penetration other than Cefalo's breakaway pass. It is an obvious passing situation, so the Dolphins go into a shotgun with Woodley deep and Harris on the left flank and Cefalo on the right. Woodley has a back blocking for him on the right and Vigorito, his most popular receiver during regular season, in the slot at the right. Should he throw, and to whom?

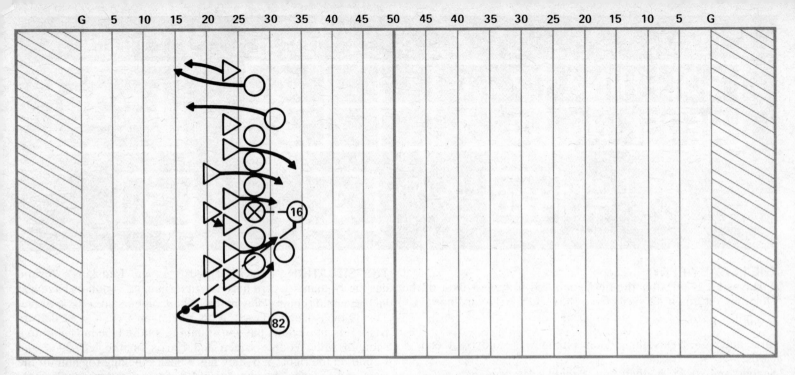

THE DECISION It is just a question of whom to make the receiver. Harris (82), going out to hook inside a few yards past the first-down marker, seems the natural choice. Woodley (16) hasn't had to try for a third-down completion yet today, so his track record is still up in the air.

THE RESULT Under a tremendous rush, Woodley got the ball to his man Harris for 7 yards and a crucial first down.

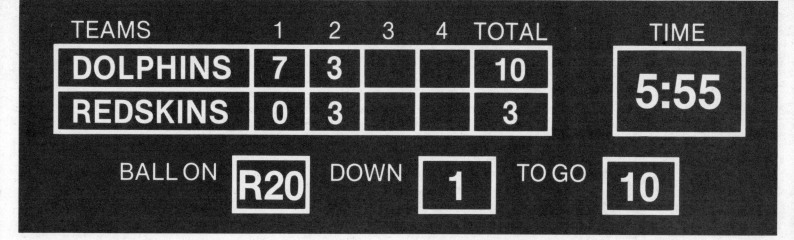

TEAMS	1	2	3	4	TOTAL
DOLPHINS	7	3			10
REDSKINS	0	3			3

TIME 5:55

BALL ON R20 DOWN 1 TO GO 10

THE PLAY-BY-PLAY

Dolphins' Ball

First and 10/R19: Franklin up the middle, 4 yards.
Second and 6/R15: Penalty, Redskins offside, 5 yards.
Second and 1/R10: Franklin up the middle, 2 yards
First and 8/R8: Franklin at right tackle, 2 yards.
Second and 6/R6: Woodley runs at right end, 3 yards.
Third and 3/R3: Woodley pass to Cefalo from shotgun, incomplete.
Fourth and 3/R3: Von Schamann kicks 20-yard field goal: Miami 10, Washington 3.
 Von Schamann kicks off to Redskin end zone; no return.

THE SITUATION The Redskins, in three possessions before this one, have only a field goal despite their obvious ability to control the ball with Riggins. Theismann has only four passes attempted, two completed, for a total of 14 yards. It has been mostly a Riggins offense, with his getting the ball on 11 of the first 18 plays from scrimmage. Setting up again with just Riggins as a setback, the Redskins are becoming a bit stereotyped. Little variety. Any ideas on how to break the mold?

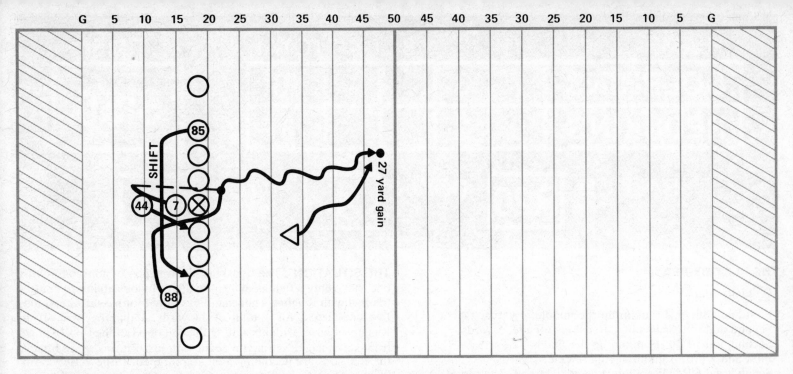

THE DECISION One of the great calls of Super Bowl XVII. After Warren (85) shifts from left tight end to the right side, Walker goes in motion, possibly to roam over to the center of the backfield near Theismann (7), then circle back to the right—the old confusion bit. But on this play, he is to slip into the line near the center and right guard and cut parallel behind the back of the scrimmage line and make a break down the left side of the field. Theismann is to make a fake handoff to Riggins (49) then find one of his receivers, possibly Walker (88).

THE RESULT Walker got free, caught the pass at the 22, and ran and bulled his way 25 more yards for a 27-yard gain. That put the Redskins at midfield.

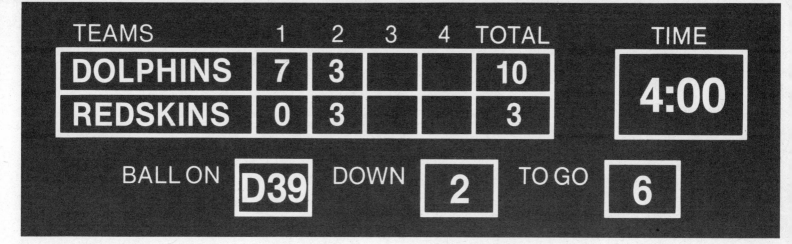

TEAMS	1	2	3	4	TOTAL	TIME
DOLPHINS	7	3			10	
REDSKINS	0	3			3	4:00

BALL ON **D39** DOWN **2** TO GO **6**

THE PLAY-BY-PLAY

Redskins' Ball

First and 10/R47: Walker takes reverse at left end, 6 yards.
Second and 4/D47: Riggins at left tackle, 3 yards.
Third and 1/D44: Riggins at left end, 1 yard.
First and 10/D43: Theismann swing pass to Brown on the right, 4 yards.

THE SITUATION

The Redskins are on the move, using more variety than in the previous drive, which earned only a field goal. Now, with a crucial second down and 6 at Miami's 39, more imagination is called for. Time is winding down in the first half, and the Redskins need a touchdown or at least another field goal going into the intermission. Riggins has been held to 5 yards on his last three attempts from scrimmage. The long passing game has not clicked yet. Miami is showing itself capable of withering a grinding-it-out team. How do you counter some of these problems?

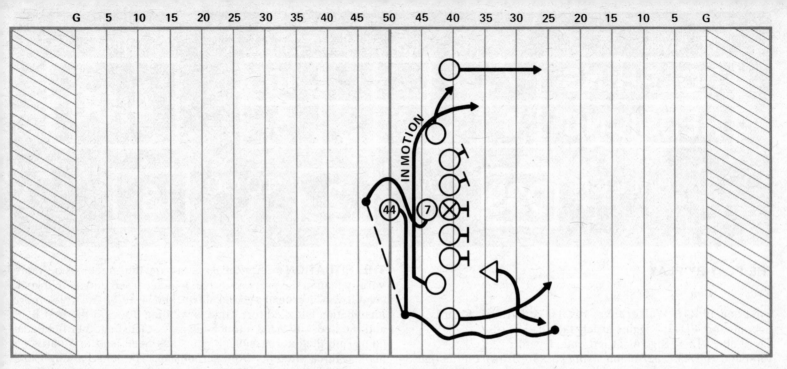

| G | 5 | 10 | 15 | 20 | 25 | 30 | 35 | 40 | 45 | 50 | 45 | 40 | 35 | 30 | 25 | 20 | 15 | 10 | 5 | G |

IN MOTION

44

7

⊗

THE DECISION To loosen up the defense on Riggins (44) and to make use of him in another way, Theismann (7) sets up in the two-tight-end, single-running-back offense. Theismann is to fade back, faking a handoff to Riggins, who lingers in the backfield. Theismann—looking for the open man—is to scramble off to the left and look for Riggins behind the line of scrimmage.

THE RESULT A nice catch and run by Riggins, who caught the ball 6 yards deep in the Redskins' backfield and rambled down the right corridor for a 15-yard first down.

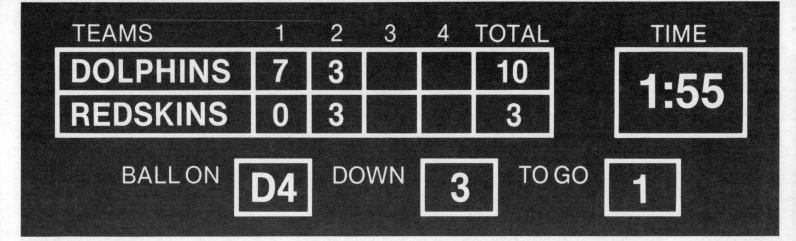

TEAMS	1	2	3	4	TOTAL	TIME
DOLPHINS	7	3			10	1:55
REDSKINS	0	3			3	

BALL ON **D4**   DOWN **3**   TO GO **1**

THE PLAY-BY-PLAY

Redskins' Ball

First and 10/D24: Riggins at right tackle, loses 1 yard.
Second and 11/D25: Theismann, back to pass, runs the right end, 12 yards.
First and 10/D13: Riggins up the middle, 6 yards.
2-minute warning.
Second and 4/D7: Riggins around left end, 3 yards.

THE SITUATION   With third down and 1 yard on Miami's 4-yard line, there is not much room to maneuver against the team that had the best defensive statistics in football during the regular season and a team that was stingy to opponents in the playoffs. Among the alternatives: go to Riggins for the yard and the first down; go to the wide receivers—Garrett and Brown—in the corner; go to the tight ends on either fancy or basic stuff; possible rollout and then a pass or run option. But Harmon replaces Riggins, so a first-down plunge by the best ballcarrier is out of the question. Giaquinto is in the slot off right tackle, but he is rarely a pass target. Try sorting out the maze as the clock is running down under two minutes.

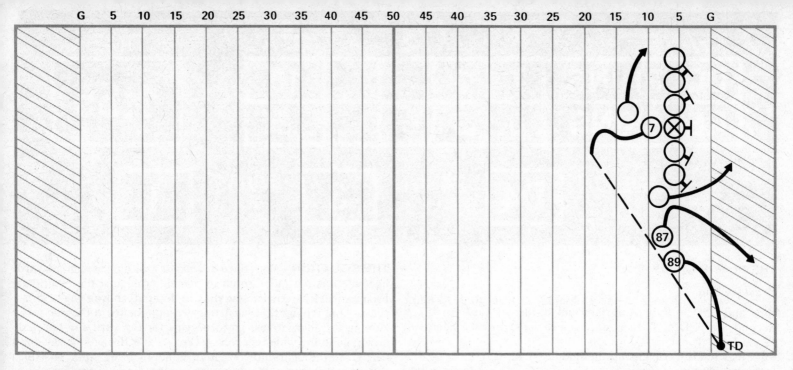

THE DECISION   Look to the right corner of the end zone, where Garrett (89) and Brown (87), who will first go in motion to the left before cutting, will be. Theismann (7) will roll slightly to the right, then loft his pass quickly to Garrett, if possible.

THE RESULT   Couldn't have been more perfect. Touchdown, Washington! Moseley made the extra point, and it was a tie game, 10-10.

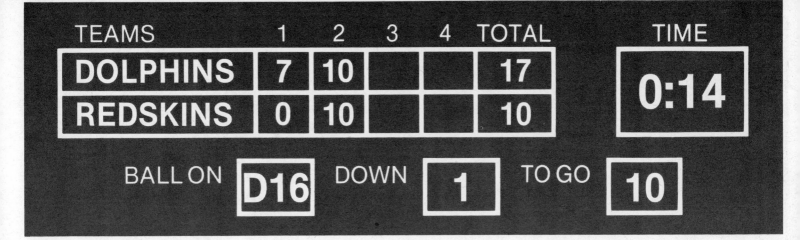

TEAMS	1	2	3	4	TOTAL	TIME
DOLPHINS	7	10			17	0:14
REDSKINS	0	10			10	

BALL ON **D16**   DOWN **1**   TO GO **10**

THE PLAY-BY-PLAY

Hayes's kickoff goes to the Dolphins' 2; from there, Fulton Walker begins to make Super Bowl history by returning the kickoff a record of 98 yards. After von Schamann makes the extra point to put the Dolphins in front again, 17–10, there is only 1 minute 38 seconds left on the clock.

Von Schamann's kickoff goes into the end zone, but Nelms returns it 20 yards to the 17. A penalty for an illegal block means that the Redskins will have to begin from their own 7-yard line, with just 1 minute 34 seconds left on the clock before halftime.

Redskins' Ball

First and 10/R7: Riggins up the middle, 3 yards.
Second and 7/R10: Harmon up the middle, 4 yards.

Third and 3/R14: Theismann, back to pass, runs the right end, 10 yards.
First and 10/R24: Theismann pass to Warren, complete, 4 yards.
Second and 6/R28: Theismann pass intended for Giaquinto, incomplete, but Miami penalized for interference. Redskins gain 30 yards on play.
First and 10/D42: Theismann pass to Brown, complete, 26 yards.

THE SITUATION With just 14 seconds remaining in the first half, the Redskins are on the Dolphins' 16-yard line with no time-outs. Moseley, the Redskin field-goal kicker, holds the league record for successive kicks but is not called into the game. Giaquinto is in the backfield, as is Harmon, which is similar to a goal-line offense. Brown sets up in back, but outside of Garrett. Warren is on the right side. A quick decision has to be made.

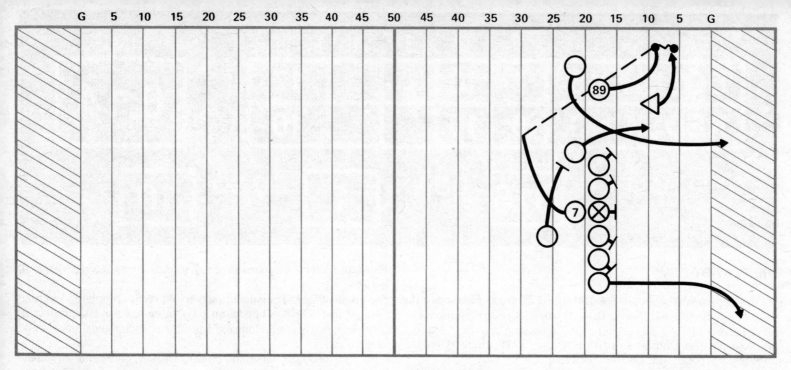

| G | 5 | 10 | 15 | 20 | 25 | 30 | 35 | 40 | 45 | 50 | 45 | 40 | 35 | 30 | 25 | 20 | 15 | 10 | 5 | G |

THE DECISION   Theismann (7) lines up his team quickly, with no time for shuffling tight ends. Theismann just wants to get a pass off, with his thoughts almost solely on Garrett (89), who can go out of bounds, giving the Redskins a short try for a field goal.

THE RESULT   Probably should have gone for the field goal in the first place. Time was too valuable with clock running out. Garrett did indeed catch the pass at the Dolphins' 8-yard line, gained another yard in a struggle, but could not get out of bounds before time ran out.

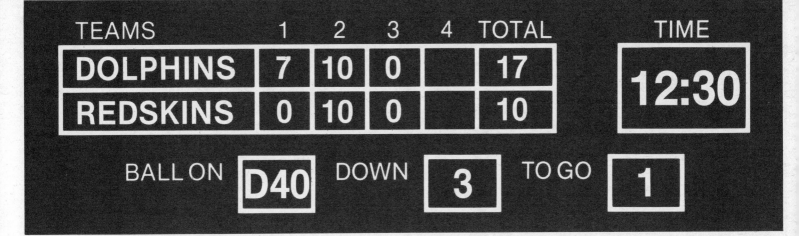

TEAMS	1	2	3	4	TOTAL	TIME
DOLPHINS	7	10	0		17	12:30
REDSKINS	0	10	0		10	

BALL ON **D40**   DOWN **3**   TO GO **1**

THE PLAY-BY-PLAY

Miami's von Schamann kicks off to the Redskin 15 to open the second half. The ball is returned to the 28 by Otis Wonsley, and a face-mask penalty advances it farther, to the 33.

Redskins' Ball

First and 10/R33: Riggins around left end, loses 1 yard.
Second and 11/R32: Theismann, sacked by Baumhower, loses 9 yards.
Third and 20/R23: Theismann pass to Brown, incomplete.
Fourth and 20/R23: Hayes punt to Dolphins' 46; fair catch by Vigorito. Dolphins penalized 15 yards for illegal block.

Dolphins' Ball

First and 10/D31: Franklin around right end, 9 yards.
Second and 1/D40: Nathan up the middle, no gain.

THE SITUATION

With third down and 1 yard to go, there are many options from this good field position. The obvious choice is for one of Miami's good runners to just go for the yard. Woodley is a strong runner, and Franklin a tough man on short yardage. Woody Bennett, who carried only nine times for 15 yards in the regular season, replaces Nathan as the other running back. At tight end and flanker are Ronnie Lee and Joe Rose, who pack extra weight. Another option is a rollout pass to the right, Woodley being a strong outside runner and the blocking strong in that direction. And, of course, many quarterbacks have been known to surprise the opposition with a bomb on third and 1. What would you call?

223

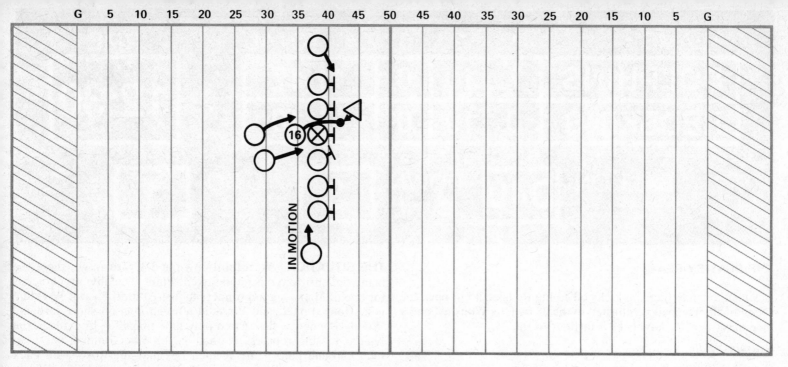

IN MOTION

THE DECISION   This is still a ball-control game and with a quarterback who has strong rushing skills, as Woodley (16) has, and a front line that includes three outstanding blockers—at center and the two guard positions—the quarterback sneak is a natural call.

THE RESULT   Woodley got the yard, but just made it. The drive is sustained.

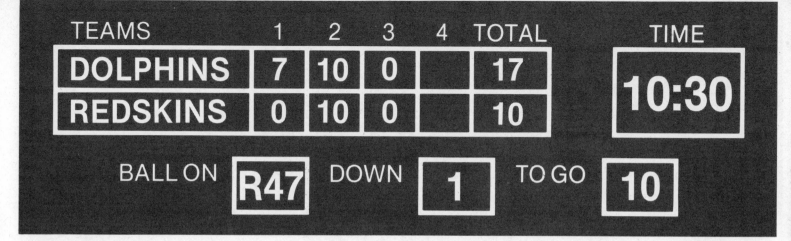

TEAMS	1	2	3	4	TOTAL
DOLPHINS	7	10	0		17
REDSKINS	0	10	0		10

TIME 10:30

BALL ON R47 DOWN 1 TO GO 10

THE PLAY-BY-PLAY

Dolphins' Ball

First and 10/D41: Woodley pass intended for Harris, incomplete.
Second and 10/D41: Franklin up the middle, 4 yards.
Third and 6/D45: Woodley pass intended for Rose, incomplete.
Fourth and 6/D45: Orosz punts 31 yards to Redskins' 24. Nelms returns it 12 yards.

Redskins' Ball

First and 10/R36: Theismann swing pass to Warren, 7 yards.
Second and 3/R43: Riggins over right tackle, 4 yards.

THE SITUATION

Redskins have first down and 10 on their own 47-yard line. Their ground game so far in the game has been effective, but in short takes. Of 19 carries by Riggins, his longest gain is 8 yards. Theismann's passing looks effective on paper, 10 of 13, but he has made good yardage to a wide receiver only once when Brown caught one for 26 yards. Two catches by Garrett have produced just 13 yards. Warren has three catches, but for short yardage. Walker has the longest catch, 27 yards, but that was a play that caught Miami off guard. What do you do—keep inching forward or go for something big?

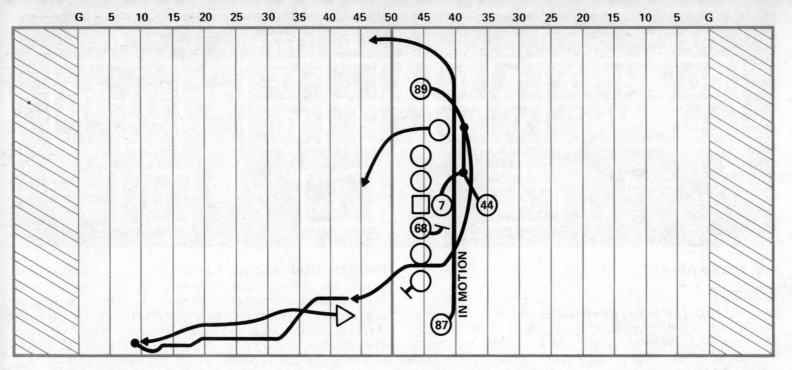

THE DECISION   Go for broke on something fancy. Brown (87) goes into motion, left to right, to create a little turmoil on a potential passing play. But Theismann (7) calls for a handoff to Riggins (44), then gives to Riggins, who heads toward right tackle. But then Riggins hands off to Garrett (89) coming around from the right.

THE RESULT   Undoubtedly one of the day's best-executed plays, perfect in timing and blocking and with extra help from left guard Russ Grimm (68). Garrett cut in sharply after passing Grimm and scampered 44 yards to the Dolphins' 9-yard line.

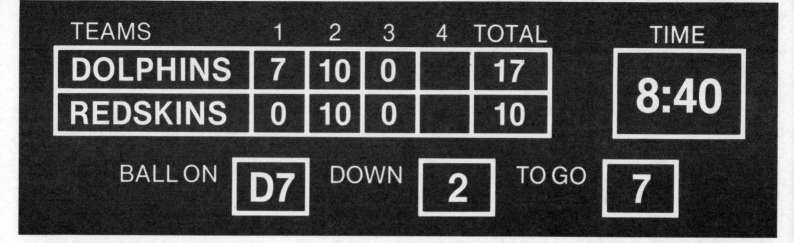

TEAMS	1	2	3	4	TOTAL
DOLPHINS	7	10	0		17
REDSKINS	0	10	0		10

TIME **8:40**

BALL ON **D7** DOWN **2** TO GO **7**

THE PLAY-BY-PLAY

Redskins' Ball

First and 9/D9: Riggins up the middle, 2 yards.

THE SITUATION   The Redskins are inside the Dolphins' 15-yard line for the fourth time today and have only one touchdown and one field goal to show for it. But no one ever said that Miami is an easy team to score on. Riggins is out on this second-down-and-7 situation. Harmon takes his place at deep back, and Giaquinto, who rarely gets the call on pass or rush plays, is also in the backfield. Warren is the tight end to the left, the speedsters Brown and Garrett to the right. Test time for Theismann. Can you supply him with any answers?

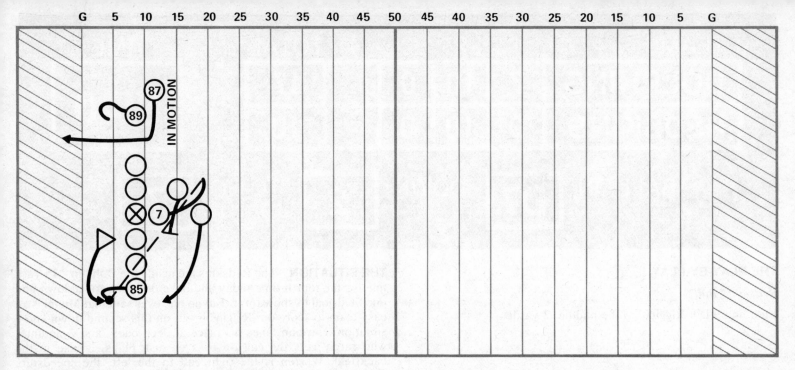

THE DECISION Theismann (7) has Brown (87) moving toward him and cutting toward the end zone, Garrett (89) hooking in, and Warren (85) going down toward the goal line with a button-hook movement. Theismann is to drop back and try to get Warren on a quick, hard pass.

THE RESULT Warren made a fine catch and bulled ahead a bit, good for 4 yards, but leaving the Redskins too far out for Riggins to ram in for a touchdown on the next play. Despite good play by Warren, Washington had put itself in a passing situation again.

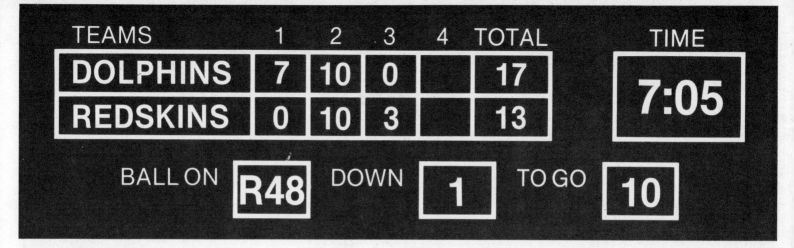

TEAMS	1	2	3	4	TOTAL
DOLPHINS	7	10	0		17
REDSKINS	0	10	3		13

TIME **7:05**

BALL ON **R48** DOWN **1** TO GO **10**

THE PLAY-BY-PLAY

Redskins' Ball

Third and 3/D3: Theismann pass to Garrett, incomplete.
Fourth and 3/D3: Moseley kicks 20-yard field goal.
Hayes's kickoff to Dolphin 14 fumbled by Lyle Blackwood and recovered and returned 15 yards by Blackwood.

Dolphins' Ball

First and 10/D29: Nathan run at left end, no gain.
Second and 10/D29: Woodley pass to Harris, incomplete.
Third and 10/D29: Woodley pass from shotgun to Vigorito, incomplete.
Fourth and 10/D29: Orosz punts to Redskin 36. Nelms returns it 12 yards.

THE SITUATION

Redskins take over on their own 48. At about midfield, they have many options. They go into a typical set, with Riggins the single running back again, plus all the good receivers—Brown, Garrett, Warren, and Walker. Theismann has many choices. So do you.

229

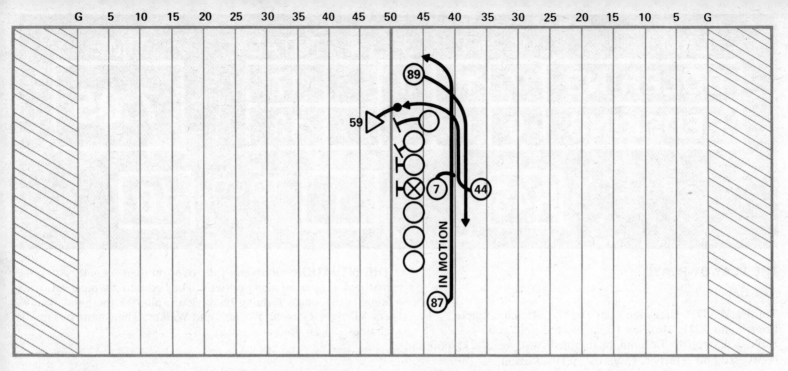

THE DECISION   The Redskins let their imagination run wild in a game in which they have called many different types of plays. This time, it is Riggins (44) on a fake reverse to Garrett (89) after Brown (87) moves left to right in motion to create some turmoil. Riggins keeps the ball and runs off Walker's shoulder.

THE RESULT   Good for only 2 yards, as Miami's left linebacker, Bob Brudzinski (59), met him head-on.

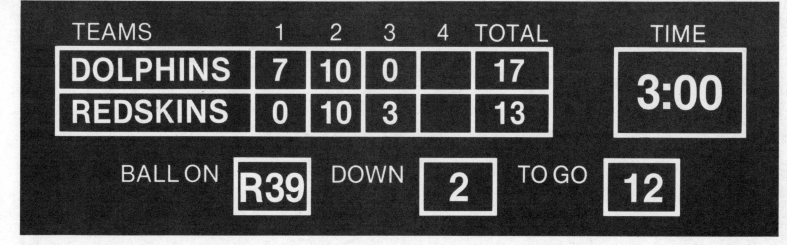

TEAMS	1	2	3	4	TOTAL	TIME
DOLPHINS	7	10	0		17	**3:00**
REDSKINS	0	10	3		13	

BALL ON R39 **DOWN** 2 **TO GO** 12

THE PLAY-BY-PLAY

Redskins' Ball

Second and 8/50: Riggins at left tackle, 2 yards.
Third and 6/D48: Theismann pass to Brown, incomplete.
Fourth and 6/D48: Hayes punts to Dolphin 6. Vigorito returns it 12 yards.

Dolphins' Ball

First and 10/D18: Franklin at left tackle, 5 yards.
Second and 5/D23: Franklin at left tackle, 1 yard.
Third and 4/D24: Woodley pass from shotgun to Harris, incomplete.
Fourth and 4/D24: Orosz punts to Redskin 30. Nelms returns it 8 yards.

Redskins' Ball

First and 10/R38: Theismann pass, intended for Warren, intercepted by Duhe at Redskin 47. No return.

Dolphins' Ball

First and 10/R47: Woodley pass to Cefalo, incomplete. Redskins offside.
First and 5/R42: Woodley, attempting to pass, runs right, 5 yards.
First and 10/R37: Franklin up the middle, loses 2 yards.

THE SITUATION   With second down and 12 yards to go, Woodley must test his passing arm if Miami is to retain the ball in what has become a tight, low-scoring game. Cefalo is wide left, Harris wide right, and the top runners—Franklin and Nathan—are in the backfield. Cefalo and Harris are the only receivers with pass-catching averages of more than 12 yards. Who do you go to if you pass?

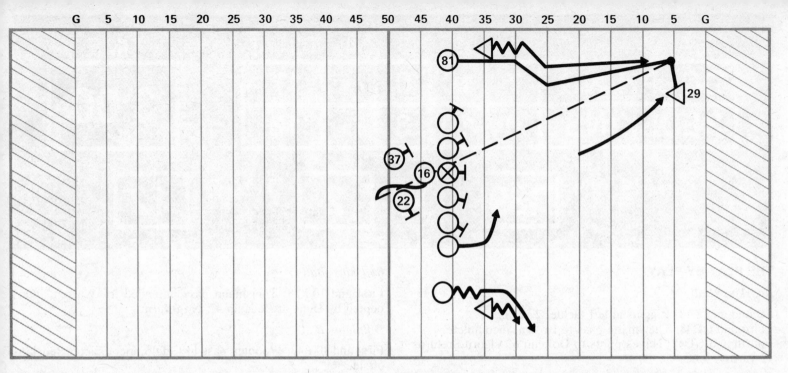

THE DECISION Woodley (16) is to drop back a little to the right, into a pocket formed by Franklin (37) and Nathan (22), and hope that Cefalo (81) can break loose over the center and get downfield near the Washington goal line.

THE RESULT Woodley put the ball in the air to Cefalo, a pass of more than 40 yards. But Cefalo tipped it, and it went off the hands of Redskins' Vernon Dean and into the hands of his teammate Mark Murphy (29) for an interception on the Redskins' 5-yard line.

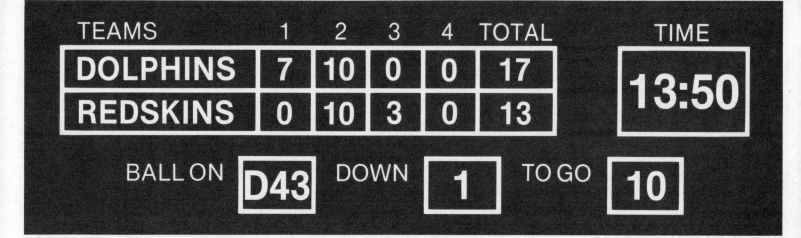

TEAMS	1	2	3	4	TOTAL	TIME
DOLPHINS	7	10	0	0	17	13:50
REDSKINS	0	10	3	0	13	

BALL ON D43   **DOWN** 1   **TO GO** 10

THE PLAY-BY-PLAY

Redskins' Ball

First and 10/R5: Riggins up the middle, 9 yards.
Second and 1/R14: Riggins up the middle, 4 yards.
First and 10/R18: Theismann pass to Brown batted in air, almost intercepted.
Second and 10/R18: Harmon up the middle, 12 yards.
First and 10/R30: Riggins up the middle, 2 yards.
Second and 8/R32: Theismann swing pass to Brown, 4 yards. End of third quarter.
Third and 6/R36: Theismann pass to Warren, 10 yards.
First and 10/R46: Riggins up the middle, 9 yards.
Second and 1/D45: Riggins over right guard, 2 yards.

THE SITUATION

The Redskins have sustained a strong drive all the way from their own 5-yard line with mostly basic plays and lots of Riggins, Riggins, Riggins. But it is still a long distance from the end-zone line, and time is winding down for a team that needs a touchdown or at least two field goals to go out in front. The touchdown is preferable, obviously, especially since the Washington attack is time-consuming and there may not be enough time to score twice on field goals if Miami has the ball in between scores. Do you agree? If so, perhaps this is the time for a big-gainer.

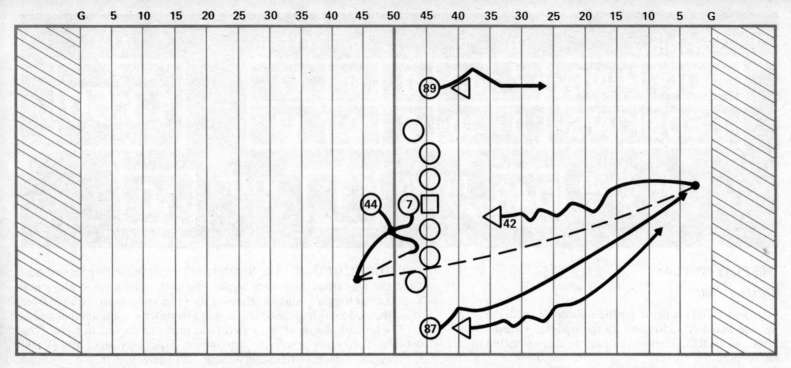

THE DECISION The Redskins indeed go for something long, and they do it in an interesting way. With Brown (87) set wide to the left, Garrett (89) set wide to the right and two tight ends in the backfield set up to the outside of the tackles, Theismann (7) drops back and hands off to Riggins (44) for what seems to be a plunge into the left side of the line. But Riggins quickly turns around to his left and laterals back to Theismann, who had continued to float back after the handoff. This eats up enough time for Brown to sprint down near the goal line and toward the middle of the field.

THE RESULT Woe, the poor Redskins! Lyle Blackwood (42) worked his way into Brown's path and intercepted for the Dolphins on their own 1-yard line. A costly turnover at this stage of the game.

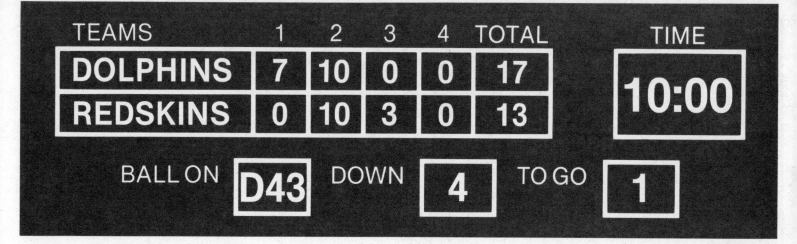

TEAMS	1	2	3	4	TOTAL	TIME
DOLPHINS	7	10	0	0	17	**10:00**
REDSKINS	0	10	3	0	13	

BALL ON **D43**   DOWN **4**   TO GO **1**

THE PLAY-BY-PLAY

Dolphins' Ball

First and 10/D1: Franklin up the middle, 2 yards.
Second and 8/D3: Franklin up the middle, 1 yard.
Third and 7 /D4: Woodley pass to Nat Moore incomplete.
Fourth and 7/D4: Orosz punts to Dolphin 45. Nelms returns it for 3 yards.
Illegal block called on Redskins' Harmon, 10-yard penalty.

Redskins' Ball

First and 10/R48: Riggins at left tackle, 7 yards.
Second and 3/D45: Riggins at left tackle, 1 yard.
Third and 2/D44: Harmon up the middle, 1 yard.

THE SITUATION The Redskins are still wary of the clock and the importance that it could play. But having controlled so much of this game, particularly the second half, with their offense, they were gaining a distinct advantage: the Dolphins' defense was getting weary from being on the field so long. Two of its star linemen, Bob Baumhower, the nose guard, and Kim Bokamper, the left end, were slightly hurt. Though it is officially fourth down and 1 yard, the actual yardage needed is only about a foot. Riggins has carried almost 30 times and only once was thrown for a loss or held to no gain. The Redskins line up in a tight, simple formation, with a second running back, Wonsley, directly in front of Riggins and Warren, the tight end, on the right side. The other man in the backfield besides Theismann, Riggins, and Wonsley is Didier, a tight end. What do you do?

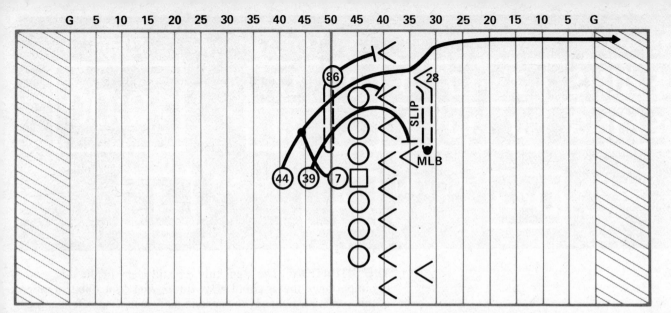

THE DECISION The Redskins, after calling a timeout, call for a somewhat routine play called a 70-Chip. Didier (86) goes in motion toward Theismann (7), then loops back toward his position. The object, as usual, is to create some confusion for the defense and make it difficult to set. But 70-Chip is just a Riggins (44) run behind the strong blocking of Wonsley (39) leading him into a hole between the left tackle and left end.

THE RESULT What should have been a first-down play became the game-breaker. As Didier went in motion, he was followed on the other side of the line by Don McNeal (28), a Dolphin cornerback. As they were running parallel, McNeal slipped when Didier made his quick cut to reverse direction. As Wonsley led Riggins through the hole and Didier turned into the Dolphin defense to provide more blocking, Riggins not only made the first-down yardage but had an open hole left by McNeal's slip when trying to reverse direction. Riggins, showing some good speed despite his workhorse day, rambled all the way to the end zone after fending off a tackle attempt by McNeal. It was a surprising effort all around, especially for Riggins, who set a record for the longest Super Bowl touchdown run on his 43-yard burst.

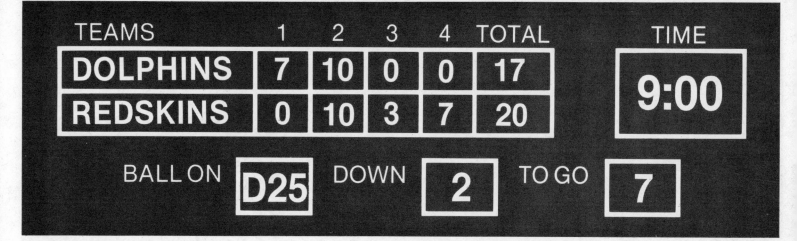

TEAMS	1	2	3	4	TOTAL
DOLPHINS	7	10	0	0	17
REDSKINS	0	10	3	7	20

TIME 9:00

BALL ON D25 **DOWN** 2 **TO GO** 7

THE PLAY-BY-PLAY

Hayes kicks off to Dolphin 8. Walker returns it 14 yards.

Dolphins' Ball

First and 10/D22: Franklin at right tackle, 3 yards.

THE SITUATION The Dolphins, behind for the first time in the game, find themselves in a difficult situation. They are better off than the Redskins were before the last touchdown, however, because they need a field goal to tie. But Woodley just isn't moving the ball. The calls don't seem to be helping him, either, as the Dolphins' staid offense has been amounting to mostly two runs and a Woodley incomplete pass on third downs. Woodley has failed five straight times to get the successful third-down pass for a first down. Then again, the Miami running game is not clicking, either. Too much Franklin-up-the-middle stuff is being diagnosed and contained by the fresh Washington defense. With an eye on the clock and a long way to go even to get into field-goal position, what do you want to do?

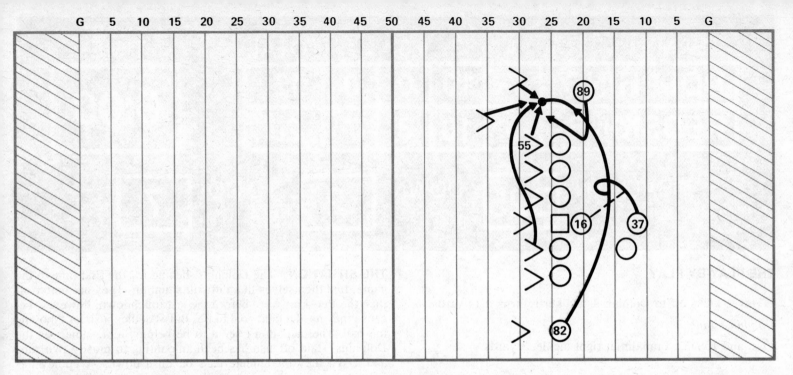

THE DECISION   Miami lines up fairly routinely, with Harris (82) split left and Moore (89) at the right wingback. Franklin (37) is the deep running back. The Dolphins call for a Woodley-to-Franklin pitchout, but Franklin pivots and hands the ball to Harris coming in motion from the left. It is a somewhat simple reverse play but one the Dolphins have not tried in the game.

THE RESULT   Reverse plays either go boom or kaput. Harris needed 7 yards but got only 1. The Redskins' Mel Kaufman (55), the left linebacker, led the waiting party for Harris when he turned in around the Dolphins' right end.

TEAMS	1	2	3	4	TOTAL	TIME
DOLPHINS	7	10	0	0	17	3:50
REDSKINS	0	10	3	7	20	

BALL ON D18   **DOWN** 3   **TO GO** 9

THE PLAY-BY-PLAY

Dolphins' Ball

Third and 6/D26: Woodley, under pressure, makes an incomplete pass. A penalty for false start costs Miami 5 yards.
Third and 11/D21: Woodley pass to Harris, incomplete.
Fourth and 11/D21: Orosz punts to Redskins' 47. Nelms returns it 12 yards.

Redskins' Ball

First and 10/D41: Riggins around left end, 6 yards.
Second and 4/D35: Riggins up the middle, 3 yards.
Third and 1/D32: Riggins over left tackle, 2 yards.
First and 10/D30: Riggins inside left tackle, 7 yards.
Second and 3/D23: Riggins up the middle, no gain.

Third and 3/D23: Harmon slants into middle, 4 yards.
First and 10/D19: Riggins up the middle, 1 yard.
Second and 9/D18: Harmon at right tackle, no gain.

THE SITUATION Redskins are virtually in a position to put the game away if they can get a touchdown. A field goal, if this particular play fails, would keep Miami from tying the game with a field goal but would put the Redskins only 6 points up and vulnerable to the Dolphins' scoring the winning touchdown. The goal-line passing team is in for Washington. Harmon replaces Riggins at the deep back. Brown and Garrett overload the left side of the line, along with Giaquinto lined up off and behind left tackle. Warren is by himself on the right side. Pretty obvious Theismann rollout left, but what does he do from there?

239

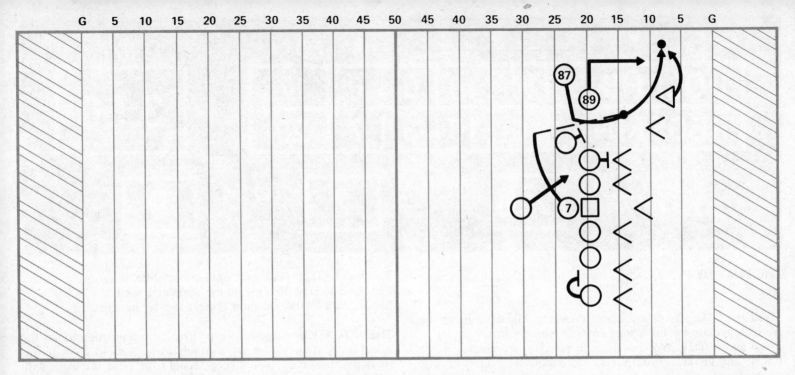

G 5 10 15 20 25 30 35 40 45 50 45 40 35 30 25 20 15 10 5 G

THE DECISION This is a nice call, with Brown (87) looping behind and to the right of Garrett (89) and heading for the sideline. Garrett takes a few steps to the left and turns straight downfield, loading the passing zone.

THE RESULT Theismann (7) rolled far to the left, which gave him a possible run or pass. His pass to Brown was on target, good enough for the first down inside the Dolphins' 10-yard line, a 9-yard gain.

2-MINUTE TIME-OUT!

One of America's favorite diversions is "Monday Night Football." But for people in the eastern time zone, the ending could almost always be called "Tuesday Morning Football." As the games on Monday begin winding down near midnight, one team or the other is usually just about to go into its 2-minute drill, milking the clock for several minutes of actual time with an endless series of timeouts, pulling away from defenders to get out of bounds, and purposely throwing incomplete passes to stop the clock.

On Monday and any other day of the week that football is played, teams have learned to utilize the final 2 minutes of the first and second halves, playing the clock for touchdowns or field goals as they do at no other juncture.

Probably no quarterback ever could work a clock like Bobby Layne, who in the 1950s led the Detroit Lions to two world championships. It was once said that "Bobby Layne never lost a game; time just ran out on him." Layne claims, however, that the genius behind his ability to play the clock was his coach, Buddy Parker, who was said to be the originator of the 2-minute drill. Layne claimed the second page in the Lions' playbook was about the 2-minute drill and that Parker would come out on the practice field with a stopwatch and make the Lions go through actual game situations under the 2-minute drill.

There were other masters of the 2-minute drill, particularly Johnny Unitas, who was also brilliant at leading a team up and down the field in the other 28 minutes of the half and thus made the final 2 minutes the climax. And there was Roger Staubach, who was said

to have brought his team from behind to win 14 times with the 2-minute strategy.

In modern times, it is nothing to cram 10 plays into the 2-minute period, keeping in mind that an average team may run only 60 to 65 plays in an entire game. After the 2-minute warning in the first half of Super Bowl XVII, Washington and Miami traded touchdowns, and those scores were followed by seven Redskins plays as Joe Theismann brought his team from his own 7-yard line to the Dolphins' 14. It took him only 1 minute 34 seconds, and then time ran out only because he didn't throw the ball out of bounds to save a field-goal attempt.

The secret of the 2-minute drill and its application to the game is (1) the use of the three timeouts alloted each team in the half and (2) play selection. Sideline passes are important because receivers can get out of bounds and stop the clock. Also, quarterbacks can throw out of bounds if a receiver is near and not worry about being penalized for intentional grounding. The time-consuming running plays—up the middle, wide sweeps—are taboo, though a good draw play can often take advantage of 2-minute defenses that play back to protect against the long pass. Playing under pressure also means having audibles called or lining up without a huddle.

What this all can mean to the fan is a game that may last an extra 20 minutes just to play 2 minutes, but it also can mean the most excitement in the entire game.

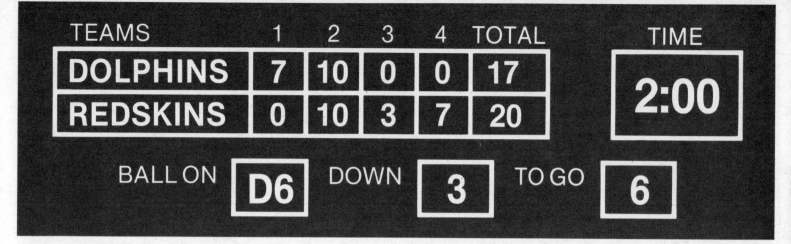

TEAMS	1	2	3	4	TOTAL	TIME
DOLPHINS	7	10	0	0	17	2:00
REDSKINS	0	10	3	7	20	

BALL ON D6 **DOWN** 3 **TO GO** 6

THE PLAY-BY-PLAY

Redskins' Ball

First and 9/D9: Riggins at left tackle, 3 yards.
Second and 6/D6: Riggins at left end, no gain.

THE SITUATION

This play may decide whether the Redskins can put the game away or have to settle for a field goal by the sure-footed Mark Moseley. The lineup is pretty much the same as the last diagramed, but this time the power is on the right side, not the left. Harmon is again in for Riggins, and Giaquinto sets up in the backfield off the right tackle, not the left. Brown and Garrett load up the right flank with top-notch receiving power. What should Theismann do in this potential game-clinching situation?

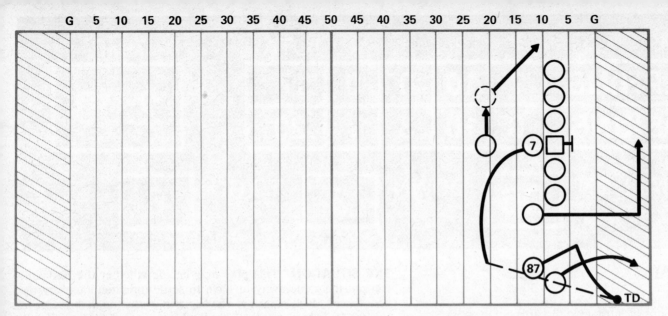

THE DECISION The call is the same as on Brown's previous 9-yard catch, though Brown (87) heads to the right corner of the end zone after looping around Garrett.

THE RESULT Theismann (7) rolled to the right, giving him the run option. But he quickly lofted the ball into the corner, and the receiver, Brown, was there to catch it. Note that this was Washington's 17th third-down situation in the game. After getting sacked in two of the first three such situations, Theismann and the Redskins have made the first down in 7 of 14 such situations as of this play. On this third down, they got the touchdown; on another, they got a touchdown on the succeeding fourth down; and on yet two others, they went on to get fourth-down field goals. For all of the many factors that were incorporated in their Super Bowl victory, the Redskins were at their best in controlling the football and wearing down the Miami defense.

TEAMS	1	2	3	4	TOTAL
DOLPHINS	7	10	0	0	17
REDSKINS	0	10	3	14	27

TIME 1:48

BALL ON **D35** DOWN **1** TO GO **10**

THE PLAY-BY-PLAY

Hayes kicks off 1 yard into Miami's end zone, and Walker returns the ball 36 yards to the Dolphin 35.

Dolphins' Ball

THE SITUATION   Don Strock replaces the ill-fated Woodley at quarterback and runs the team from the shotgun offense, with the Redskins well prepared for a flurry of passes with less than 2 minutes in the game. Strock has Harris wide left, Cefalo wide right, and in the backfield, Tom Vigorito at left halfback and Tony Nathan at right halfback. It is a first-and-10 situation, and there is no time to spare. What do you call?

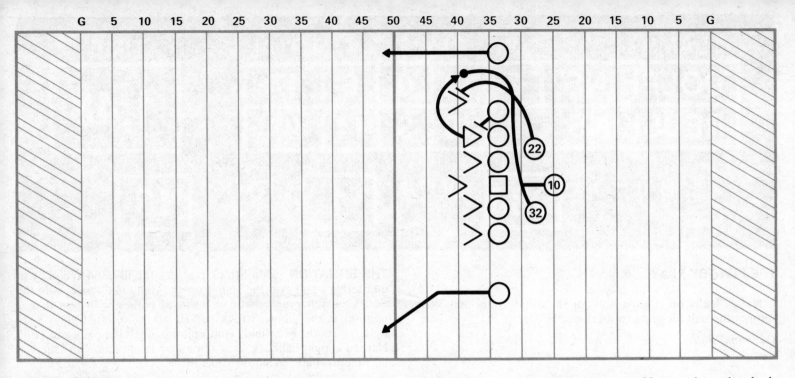

THE DECISION This call was one for the second-guessers. Instead of a pass, Strock (10) called for a handoff to Vigorito (32), cutting in front of him and picking up Nathan's (22) block to run the right end.

THE RESULT A 4-yard gain that ate up 23 seconds on the clock.

THE REMAINING PLAY-BY-PLAY OF SUPER BOWL XVII

Dolphins' Ball

Second and 6/D39: Strock pass to Cefalo, incomplete.
Third and 6/D39: Strock pass to Vigorito, incomplete.
Fourth and 6/D39: Strock pass to Harris, incomplete.

Redskins' Ball

First and 10/D39: Harmon up the middle, 3 yards.
Second and 7/D36: Harmon at left guard, 4 yards.
Third and 3/D32: Harmon at left tackle, cutting to middle, 4 yards.
First and 10/D28: Theismann falls back on the ball, loses 2 yards.

END OF GAME

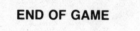

SUPER BOWL SUPERLATIVES

All-Time Super Bowl Records

SCORING

Most Points (Lifetime): 24, Franco Harris, Pittsburgh, 4 games

Most Points (One Game): 15, Don Chandler, Green Bay, 1968

Most Touchdowns (Lifetime): 4, Franco Harris, Pittsburgh, 4 games

Most Touchdowns (Game): 2, Shared by 9 players

Most Points After Touchdown (Lifetime): 8, Don Chandler, Green Bay, 2 games; Roy Gerela, Pittsburgh, 3 games

Most Points After Touchdown (Game): Don Chandler, Green Bay, 1967; Roy Gerela, Pittsburgh, 1979

Most Field Goals (Lifetime): 4, Don Chandler, Green Bay, 2 games; Jim Turner, Jets and Denver, 2 games; Ray Wersching, San Francisco, 1 game

Most Field Goals (Game): 4, Don Chandler, Green Bay, 1968; Ray Wersching, San Francisco, 1982

Longest Field Goal: 48, Jan Stenerud, Kansas City, 1970

Longest Touchdown: 98, Fulton Walker, Miami, 1983 (kickoff return)

RUSHING

Most Attempts (Lifetime): 101, Franco Harris, Pittsburgh, 4 games

Most Attempts (Game): 38, John Riggins, Washington, 1983

Most Yards Gained (Lifetime): 354, Franco Harris, Pittsburgh, 4 games

Most Yards Gained (Game): 166, John Riggins, Washington, 1983

Longest Gain: 58, Tom Matte, Baltimore, 1969

Longest Gain for Touchdown: 43, John Riggins, Washington, 1983

PASSING

Most Attempts (Lifetime): 98, Roger Staubach, Dallas, 4 games

Most Attempts (Game): 38, Ron Jaworski, Philadelphia, 1981

Most Completions (Lifetime): 61, Roger Staubach, Dallas, 4 games

Most Completions (Game): 25, Ken Anderson, Cincinnati, 1982

Highest Completion Percentage (Lifetime): 63.6, Len Dawson, Kansas City, 2 games

Highest Completion Percentage (Game): 73.5, Ken Anderson, Cincinnati, 1982

Most Yards Gained (Lifetime): 932, Terry Bradshaw, Pittsburgh, 4 games

Most Yards Gained (Game): 318, Terry Bradshaw, Pittsburgh, 1979

Longest Completion: 80, Jim Plunkett, Oakland, 1981 (touchdown)

Most Touchdown Passes (Lifetime): 9, Terry Bradshaw, Pittsburgh, 4 games

Most Touchdown Passes (Game): 4, Terry Bradshaw, Pittsburgh, 1979

Most Interceptions (Game): 4, Craig Morton, Denver, 1978

PASS RECEIVING

Most Receptions (Lifetime): 16, Lynn Swann, Pittsburgh, 4 games

Most Receptions (Game): 11, Dan Ross, Cincinnati, 1982

Most Yards Gained (Lifetime): 364, Lynn Swann, Pittsburgh, 4 games

Most Yards Gained (Game): 161, Lynn Swann, Pittsburgh, 1976

Longest Reception: 80, Kenny King, Oakland, 1981 (touchdown)

INTERCEPTIONS

Most Interceptions (Lifetime): 3, Chuck Howley, Dallas, 2 games; Rod Martin, Oakland, 1 game

Longest Return: 75, Willie Brown, Oakland, 1977 (touchdown)

PUNTING

Most Punts (Game): 9, Ron Widby, Dallas, 1971

Highest Average (Game): 48.5, Jerrel Wilson, Kansas City, 1970 (4 punts)

Longest Punt: 61, Jerrel Wilson, Kansas City, 1970

PUNT RETURNS

Most Punt Returns (Game): 6, Mike Nelms, Washington, 1983

Most Yards (Game): 53, Mike Nelms, Washington, 1983

Longest Return: 31, Willie Wood, Green Bay, 1968

KICKOFF RETURNS

Most Kickoff Returns (Game): 5, Larry Anderson, Pittsburgh, 1980; Billy Campfield, Philadelphia, 1981; David Verser, Cincinnati, 1982

Most Yards (Game): 190, Fulton Walker, Miami, 1983

Longest Return: 98, Fulton Walker, Miami, 1983 (touchdown)

TEAM RECORDS—ONE GAME

Scoring: 35, Green Bay, 1967; Pittsburgh, 1979

First Downs: 24, Cincinnati, 1982; Washington, 1983

First Downs Rushing: 15, Dallas, 1972

First Downs Passing: 15, Minnesota, 1977; Pittsburgh, 1979

Net Yards Gained: 429, Oakland, 1977

Rushing Yards Gained: 276, Washington, 1983

Passing Yards Gained: 309, Pittsburgh, 1980

Rushes Attempted: 57, Pittsburgh, 1975

Passes Attempted: 44, Minnesota, 1977

Passes Completed: 25, Cincinnati, 1982

Most Interceptions (of opponents): 4, Jets, 1969; Dallas, 1978

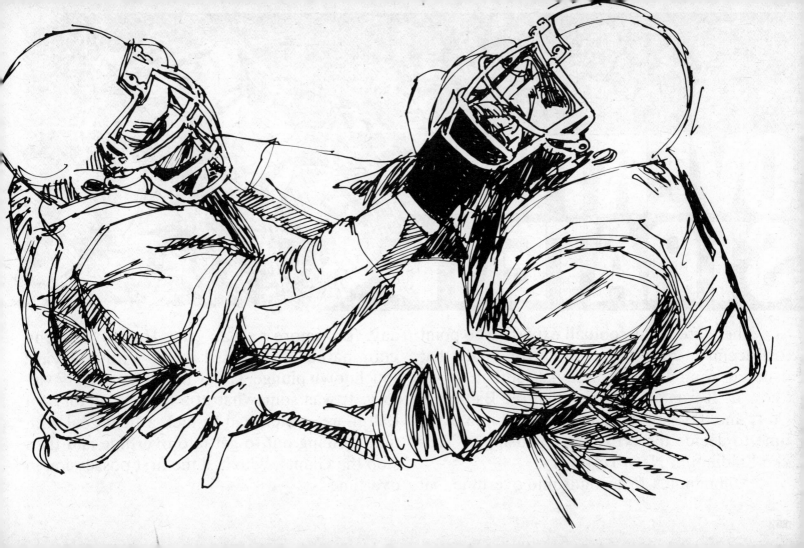

OVERTIME STRATEGY

There are many football experts who point to December 28, 1958, as the pivotal date that ushered in modern professional football as we know it. It was on that date that the Baltimore Colts and the New York Giants went into overtime to decide the NFL championship at Yankee Stadium in New York City.

At 8 minutes 15 seconds into overtime that day, Baltimore's Alan (the Horse) Ameche culminated an 80-yard drive with a 1-yard touchdown plunge, giving the Colts a 23–17 victory. It was somewhat of a miracle victory for Baltimore, which had to kick a field goal with time running out to get into overtime and then stop the Giants, who had the first possession in overtime.

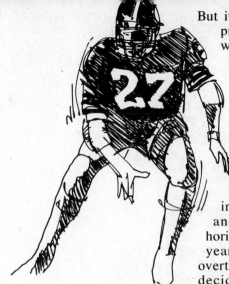

But it was a bigger victory for professional football, which was just entering the era of national television and could not have given 64,000 fans at Yankee Stadium and an audience across the country a better showcase event. Within two years, the AFL, taking advantage of growing pro-football interest whetted in that game, would form and expand pro football's horizons. In fact, in just four years after the Giants-Colts overtime game, the AFL, too, decided its championship in overtime as the Dallas Texans (now the Kansas City Chiefs) defeated the Houston Oilers, 20-17. That game became known as "football's longest day" because the Texans needed 17 minutes 54 seconds before they could kick a field goal to decide the championship. No pro game before that time had lasted longer in actual playing time.

In the next few years, there would be two more overtime thrillers to decide playoff games. In 1965, the Green Bay Packers defeated Baltimore, 16-10, in 13 minutes 39 seconds of extra play to win the NFL's Western Conference title. Then, on Christmas Day, 1971, the Miami Dolphins defeated Kansas City, 27-24, in 22 minutes 40 seconds of overtime, revising the record for "football's longest day" in an AFC divisional playoff game.

All of these games, of course, were played under some kind of postseason playoff situation, in which a stalemate is not possible, as were two other overtime playoff games (Oakland Raiders 37, Baltimore 31, at 15:43 overtime in the American Conference divisional playoffs, December 24, 1977; San Diego Chargers 41, Miami 38, at 13:52 of overtime in the American Conference divisional playoffs on January 2, 1982).

But in 1974, after more than 4,000 regular-season games had been played in NFL history, the league decided to install the overtime rule for regular-season games, too, the only variance being that a tie would be declared if neither team scored in the alloted 15 minutes' extra time.

With that innovation, the 28 teams of the NFL had to begin thinking overtime strategy well before the usual December playoff games began.

Do you go for the field goal at the first opportunity, or can you think touchdown?

Are you dead in such a sudden-death overtime if you don't win the coin flip and get the first possession?

Do you *have to score* the first time you get the ball after winning the toss?

In the nine seasons since the overtime rule was instituted, there have been 72 such regular-season games, and some patterns have emerged that may have surprised coaches and fans alike.

The Pittsburgh Steelers played the Denver Broncos to a 35-35 tie in the first game played under the new rule on September 22, 1974. The two teams got conservative in overtime, to the detriment of each. It would become one of six overtime situations.

After their tie, the Steelers became masters of the overtime, winning five straight times.

The Steelers alone, with their brilliant quarterback Terry Bradshaw at the controls, had answered at least one question: you don't have to take the easy way out and plan around a field goal.

In fact, in its most recent overtime victory, the Steelers could have easily used the field goal to put away the Bengals in a crucial early-season game. The Bengals had won the toss in that game, but the tough, blitzing Steelers forced an interception on third and 6 and Dwayne Woodruff, a Steeler cornerback, returned the ball to Cincinnati's 2-yard line.

The Steelers called a timeout to discuss strategy, though it seemed obvious that a quick field goal at that point would have been much simpler.

Bradshaw told Steeler Coach Chuck Noll to go for the field goal, but Noll wanted one of his running backs to try to bull the ball over on an inside plunge. Bradshaw spoke up again, however, telling his coach: "Well, let me throw it, then. We could get a fumble on a running play." At least with a pass, Bradshaw figured, he could throw the ball out of bounds or past the end zone and the Steelers still would have three more tries.

The coach agreed, calling for a pass play to the wide receiver on the right, John Stallworth, with a possible option run by Bradshaw. The ball was snapped, Bradshaw rolled right, Stallworth went to the inside and then turned out, and Bradshaw had an easy target. Stallworth made the catch at 1 minute 8 seconds into the overtime. The Steelers won the game, 26–20.

The result, according to an updated version of an NFL study in 1982, should not have been too surprising.

Of 72 overtime games in regular season since the 1974 debut of the new rule, here are some of the facts:

In 52 games, both teams had possession at least one time in overtime (or 72 percent of the games played). In 35 games, the team that won the toss won the game (a surprising 48.6 percent, though one would wonder if any coach would dare refuse to receive, given the choice). In 20 games, the team that won the toss drove for the winning score (27.8 percent). In 19 games, the winning score was by a touchdown (26.3 percent). In 47 games, the winning margin was by a field goal (65.3 percent). In 6 games, there were ties (8.3 percent).

Ties, of course, are the longest overtime games because they are declared if no one scores within the extra 15 minutes. But the shortest overtime game took only 21 seconds. That is how long it took the Detroit Lions' kickoff to get to the Chicago Bears' David Williams and for Williams to return the kick 95 yards for a touchdown on November 27, 1980.

The NFL survey pointed out that all 28 of the league's teams have shared in the excitement of overtime regular-season games since 1974. But not all have done equally well. Here is how the teams have done in regular-season sudden-death games, best to worse:

NFC

AFC

WON
LOST
TIED

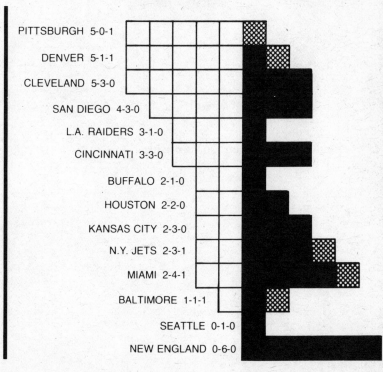

WASHINGTON 5-2-0
CHICAGO 4-5-0
L.A. RAMS 3-1-1
DALLAS 3-2-0
SAN FRANCISCO 3-2-0
MINNESOTA 3-2-2
TAMPA BAY 2-0-1
ST. LOUIS 2-4-0
N.Y. GIANTS 2-4-0
ATLANTA 2-4-0
GREEN BAY 1-1-3
DETROIT 0-2-0
PHILADELPHIA 0-2-0
NEW ORLEANS 0-3-0

PITTSBURGH 5-0-1
DENVER 5-1-1
CLEVELAND 5-3-0
SAN DIEGO 4-3-0
L.A. RAIDERS 3-1-0
CINCINNATI 3-3-0
BUFFALO 2-1-0
HOUSTON 2-2-0
KANSAS CITY 2-3-0
N.Y. JETS 2-3-1
MIAMI 2-4-1
BALTIMORE 1-1-1
SEATTLE 0-1-0
NEW ENGLAND 0-6-0

255